The Certified Application Development Manager

Copyright © 2020 Zulk Shamsuddin, PhD

GAFM ACADEMY

All rights reserved.

ISBN: 9798302063588

INTRODUCTION

The **Certified Application Development Manager (CADM)** is a gold-standard certification accredited by the Global Academy of Finance and Management ®. This credential is for individuals with skills and experience in planning, coordinating, and supervising all activities related to an organization's software applications to keep businesses running smoothly. CADM-Certified professionals are experienced in the design, development, testing, and implementation of software applications, project management, change management, and quality management, and possess communication and organizational leadership skills.

It forms the basis of the assessment that applicants must pass to gain the Certified Application Development Manager status and inclusion in the Directory of Certified Professionals of The GAFM Academy of Finance and Management ®.

Stand out from the crowd with the GAFM® Certified Application Development Manager certification and publish the title "CADM" after your name.

INTERNATIONAL BOARD OF STANDARDS CERTIFYING BODY

GAFM IBS International Board of Standards Certifying Body operate in over 40 nations worldwide and have members in over 150 countries. The IBS owns the certifications and trademarks conferred by the GAFM Global Academy of Finance and Management ® and The American Academy of Project Management ®. Our International Board of Standards Accreditation council is located in the EU and USA. Our Certification Body and Governance Team regulates the standards for certification and accredited education criteria for qualified training and degree programs which are a direct path to our certifications. The Board of Standards awards designations and board certification in the finance, accounting, risk, economics, and management consulting areas. The IBS is EU Accredited in Europe and ISO Certified for Quality and Training under ISO 21001 Standards. The IBS is a charter member signatory to the Higher Education Quality Standards Commission and a global standards agreement with the USA Accreditation agency ACBSP Accreditation Council for Business Schools and Programs and has been recognized on the AACSB website by the President. The IBS owns over 30 trademark certification brands and licenses the certifications to members around the world. Over 20 years of unmatched quality standards working with business schools worldwide.

Certified Application Development Manager

The U.S. Bureau of Labor Statistics (BLS) reports that overall employment of computer software engineers and computer programmers, the category that includes application development managers, is expected to be very strong in coming years. Demand for application development managers will increase as electronic data processing systems used in business, finance, healthcare, government and other settings become more complex. As the need for computer software and specialty applications grows, the demand for application development managers should increase.

Job Duties for Application Development Managers

Application development managers are typically responsible for a team that monitors, analyzes, designs and develops a company's computer software applications. They are also usually in charge of maintaining, supporting, and upgrading existing systems and applications needed to keep the business running.

Other job duties include managing development projects to ensure they meet the company's business requirements and goals, as well as working with other departments to establish their software needs. Application development managers often test new software programs and applications, assist with quality assurance, and identify and resolve program issues and errors.

Some application development managers may report to a company's chief information officer. Most supervise workers; staff size generally varies according to the size of the firm. When planning and directing projects with a team, the application development manager will assign work, review and evaluate performance, and meet with staff to identify and solve problems.

The road to an application development manager career can begin with a bachelor's degree in business administration with a concentration in computer information systems. Coursework typically includes system analysis and design, database concepts and programming, organization theory and electronic commerce.

Employers can be confident that graduates of a business administration program with a concentration in computer information systems are able to:

- Streamline information systems and processes.
- Apply network theory and design principles to real-world scenarios.
- Demonstrate the technical expertise necessary for today's complex business needs.
- Assist with strategic planning and manage a team of software application specialists.
- Leverage advanced skills and knowledge to succeed as an application development manager.

Who should read this book?

Anyone with the required minimum qualifications and the necessary experience associated with software development should consider getting certified by reading this book.

- Golden opportunity for Graduates and Professionals.
- Getting shortlist for a job opportunity.
- Applicants with a certified credential are usually the preferred choice among top recruiters and employers.
- Candidate with certification earn attractive compensation package comparatively with others with similar job.
- Recognized credibility.
- Greater employment prospects across the globe.
- Leveraging international quality accreditation (ISO Standards) to your name, and CV.

- Get recognition of your skills and competencies as specified on the accredited endorsement training certificate.

- Leveraging the certification card to establish professional relationship during social networking, corporate events, seminars, conferences, trainings, et cetera.

- Get listed in the GAFM® Directory of Certified and Chartered Professionals.

Build your Dreams, Get Certified

Certificates and certifications, the names for these credentials sound confusingly similar. But there are important differences. Here's what you need to know about these resume-enhancing options and how they might advance your career.

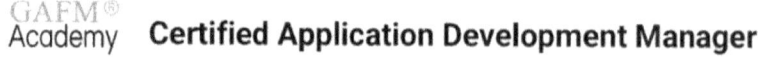

Certification will differentiate you from the crowd, from thousands of applications eyeing on that single job opening, your profile stands tall above the rest! You will be asking yourself – what makes you so special? How could a single piece of paper make a difference? What about the bachelor's degree certificate? Some of the candidates are better than you but why aren't they shortlisted?

You may think that since you have secured a job, getting certified is optional. When you are out of job for whatever reasons, retrenchment, corporate downsizing, economic downturn, office politics, et cetera then you start to feel the pressure to secure another job. Competition is intense out there, connections come handy but not everyone has strong cable these days. When you look at job adverts, although they did not explicitly mention that you must be certified to apply for the job opening, they do filter candidates based on these criteria when it comes to shortlist thousands of candidates.

So, you are left out of the opportunity to compete in the job marketplace! Then you start rushing to get certified. It's a little too late. By that time, the certification fee has gone up.

If you do not have working experience then it is highly unlikely you will be offered to sit for any certification courses. This put fresh graduates in a highly difficult position. If you have the ambition to work abroad, you need to have at least one accredited and globally recognized certification to apply for jobs abroad being in the US, Europe, Middle East or elsewhere. If you don't have this, it is highly unlikely that you will get your application shortlisted.

(actual certificates in your name with certified seal emblem)

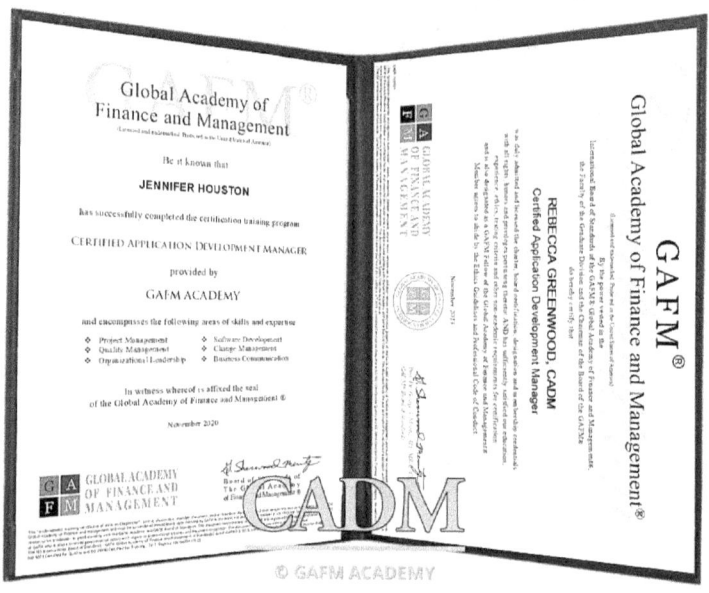

Benefits of becoming a Certified Application Development Manager

- Personal and International recognition.
- An ISO-standard top-quality certification.
- Enhanced your CV and get noticed by top recruiters.
- The best platform for the development of your professional career.
- Assurance for clients of high standards and ethical practice.
- Use of the post-nominal designation after your name
- Increased understanding, helping you to work more effectively.
- Use the elegant certification card during networking or social events.

Why you need to get certified?

When you have the professional knowledge you need, a certification allows you to prove it. Certifications indicate mastery of skills or standards. Professional certifications are granted by industry groups or career-related organizations. These groups assess your qualifications, usually through an exam or application process. Many certifications include the privilege to use a related designation following your professional title. A professional certification differs from a license, which permits you to work in a certain profession and is usually issued by government or regulatory agencies.

Certification is about verifying your experience against a set of skills and competencies that are related to the specific job or role. Obviously you need to have the appropriate level of knowledge associated with the skills. You also need to have the minimum qualification (bachelor degree) and higher as a prerequisite for any certification.

KNOWLEDGE + QUALIFICATION + EXPERIENCE
are the cornerstones of GAFM® Certifications

Examination is not only based upon your knowledge, skills and competencies but also the methodologies, processes, and the industry standards that you need to know and practice in your past experience. At GAFM Academy, we provide an eBook to facilitate the examination process so that the assessments are aligned with the skills and competencies pertaining to the specific certification.

Click the link below to apply

https://shorturl.at/cES36

THE VALUE OF CERTIFICATION

- Certification helps in learning new technologies, skills, and abilities for a specific promotion. Earning a new certification or an advanced certification in a particular area of expertise can help in advancing your career.

- Professional certification shows consumers and potential employers that you are committed to your profession and are well-trained. It gives them confidence in your abilities and knowledge.

- Certification makes you more valuable to employers, so you can expect to earn more than someone without certification.

- Certifications can give you the chance to learn needed skills, and be a quick way to show employers you have those skills. On the other hand, certifications can require studying or coursework, and cost up to several hundred dollars to take.

FREQUENTLY ASKED QUESTIONS

Why do I need to submit a CV?

We only accept candidates who meet the minimum qualification requirements and credible work experience.

When will GAFM process my application?

Application will only be processed after payment is received.

How do I pay?

We accept payments via Credit / Debit card. Payment link will be shared once your application has been accepted.

Can I pay via bank wire transfer?

Yes, we will share the invoice with banking details.

How do I prepare myself for the exam?

This is a self-study model. An eBook will be provided, examination will be based on the information in the eBook. The eBook will be provided FREE to successful candidates after payment has been made.

How long is the duration of self-study period?

You must complete this study period inclusive of the exam within ten days from the date of payment.

How do I write the exam?

When you're ready to write the exam, kindly email us to book your schedule for the exam.

How do I apply for exemption from the exam?

This is at the discretion of the Board. You may be requested to submit additional information in addition to the CV submitted earlier. In any case, if your experience is good, we will apply for an exemption only after payment has been received.

How is the exam structured?

The examination comprised of 40 multiple choice questions.
Difficulty: Moderate   Duration: 60 minutes

What is the passing grade?
70%

When will I know the result of the exam?
Within 48 hours

What if I failed in the first attempt?
You are allowed to rewrite the exam without any additional charge.

When will I receive the certification documents?
Shipping is within 10 business days after you complete the course.

What are the certification documents?
i) professional accredited certificate   ii) endorsement training certificate   iii) certification card

Can I get a digital copy of the certificates?
We do not issue digital copy.

What is the endorsement training certificate?
This is the certificate that indicate the skills and competencies associated with the professional accredited certificate where you have accomplished via the online training program.

Can I apply the designation after my name while waiting for the certification documents?

Yes

Chapter 1 : SOFTWARE DEVELOPMENT LIFE CYCLE

The information systems (IS) project is a component of an information technology (IT) project. An IT project comprised of servers, networks, data centers, databases, storage, and many others including applications that are also called "software or systems".

This book focuses on project management associated with application development specifically the processes that will be used to implement software development projects. There are several methods available today to manage a software project, the decision to adopt a particular method is dependent upon several factors which include budget, schedule, quality and customer requirements. This book focuses on the method to manage software development projects using the SDLC model which is comprised of six phases that include system initiation, system requirements, system design, system construction, system acceptance, and system implementation. This book will guide you to manage information systems projects from ground zero using a structured methodology that will guide you to take on any information systems project with confidence.

SYSTEM INITIATION

The Business Case and proposed solution developed during project conceptual phase are re-examined to ensure that they are still relevant and address an existing organizational need. This validation effort provides the Project Team with the basis for a detailed schedule defining the steps needed to obtain a thorough understanding of the business requirements and an initial view of staffing needs. In addition, a high-level schedule is developed for subsequent phases of the system development life cycle (SDLC).

System Requirements

The needs of the business are captured in as much detail as possible. The Project Manager leads the Project Team in working with the Customers to define what it is that the new system must do. By obtaining a detailed and comprehensive understanding of the business requirements, the Project Team can develop the Functional Specification that will drive the system design.

System Design

The Functional Specification developed during System Requirements phase will be used as input into the development of a complete technical solution. This solution dictates the technical architecture, standards, specifications and strategies to be followed throughout the building, testing, and implementation of the system. The completion of System Design also marks the point in the project at which the Project Manager should be able to plan, in detail, all future project phases.

System Construction

This is the phase throughout which the Project Team build and test the various modules of the application, including any utilities that will be needed during System Acceptance and System Implementation. As system components are built, they will be tested both individually and in logically related and integrated groupings until such time as a full system test has been performed to validate functionality. Documentation and training materials are also developed during this phase.

System Acceptance

This phase focuses on system validation efforts that shift from those team members responsible for developing the application to those who will ultimately use the system in the execution of their daily responsibilities. In addition to confirming that the system meets functional expectations, activities are aimed at validating all aspects of data conversion and system deployment.

SYSTEM IMPLEMENTATION

The final phase of the SDLC which comprises all activities associated with the deployment of the application. These efforts include training, installation of the system in a production setting, and transition of ownership of the application from the Project Team to the Customer. The final process is the closure of a project which should include contract closure and administrative closure. Contract closure ensures that all of the deliverables and agreed-upon terms of the project have been completed and delivered so that the project can end. It allows resources to be reassigned and settlement or payment of any account, if applicable.

System Development Life Cycle

INITIATION	REQUIREMENTS	DESIGN	CONSTRUCTION	ACCEPTANCE	IMPLEMENTATION
Prepare for System Initiation	Prepare for Requirements Analysis	Define Technical Architecture	Prepare DEV Environment	Prepare UAT Environment	Prepare PRODUCTION Environment
Establish Project Team	Collect Business Requirements	Define System Standards	Build, Test, & Validate	Validate Data Conversion	System Deployment
Define Scope	Define Process Model	Database Design	Prepare SIT Environment	Execute User Acceptance Testing	Conduct Training
Define Cost	Define Logical Data Model	Prototype System Components	Conduct System Integration Testing	Update Project Documentations	Transition Management
Identify Risk	Map Requirements / Model	Develop Testing Strategy	Develop Project Documentations	System Acceptance	Project Closeout
Define Quality	Produce Functional Specification	Validate Work Package	Develop Training Material		
Develop Project Charter	Develop High-Level Project Management Plan	Develop Project Management Plan			

Project management execution and controlling functions which include communications management, risk management, scope management, issues management, and project team management are being applied throughout the various phases of the system development life cycle, these are described from Chapter 7 onwards.

WHY CUSTOM-BUILT APPLICATIONS?

Any company will need an accounting system, payroll system, human resource management system, enterprise resource planning system, or any business applications to improve efficiency and increases productivity in addition to seamless communication with their customers they interact with. These applications were developed from scratch back in the early 80s as limited vendors are supplying off-the-shelve software at that time. In the early 90s, several software companies are offering standard off-the-shelf business applications that can deliver the solutions within a shorter period. However, there is no such thing as "one size fits all", customization is imminent when dealing with enterprises in the digital economy. These applications were installed to include other requirements and usually, the implementations require some customization effort. Despite all these, other applications need to be developed from ground zero simply because the business processes that support the enterprise functional operations are unique to that organization where standard off-the-shelf applications are scarce or they do not provide the functionalities required. So, you need people like Systems Analyst, Analyst Programmer, Solution Architect, Software Tester, and others to deliver the custom-designed applications.

SDLC is by far still the best method to build software from the ground up. The six phases of the SDLC are discussed in the following chapters.

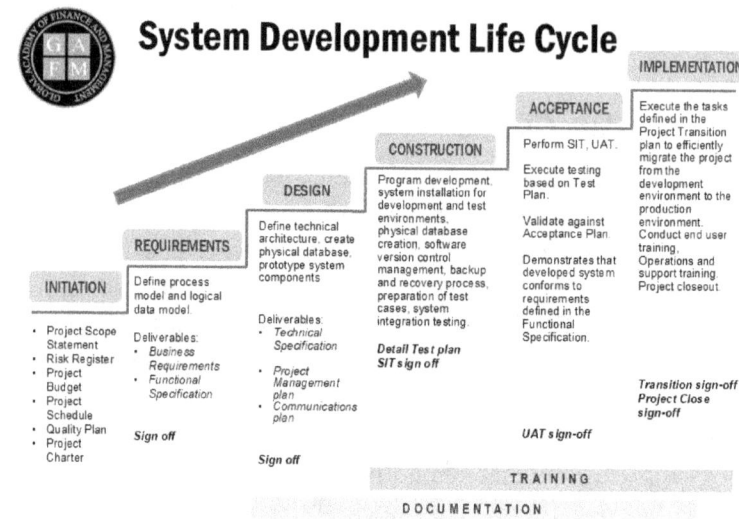

Chapter 2 : SYSTEM INITIATION

The purpose of System Initiation is to validate the proposed solution developed during the conceptual phase of the project management life cycle and to estimate the system development effort in greater detail. In this phase, the broad parameters of the new system are defined, and applicable system development activities are identified.

Once the overall approach has been confirmed, it is necessary to estimate the effort and resources required for the next phase in elemental detail and to provide high-level estimates for subsequent phases, to the extent necessary to support the system development life cycle deliverables and activities of System Initiation.

System Initiation

Objective:
- To define the overall requirements and deliverables of a project
- To establish the high-level project plan required to complete the project
- To kick off the project.

Output:
- Project Charter
- Preliminary Project Plan

THE PEOPLE

The following roles are involved in carrying out the processes of this phase. Detailed descriptions of these roles can be found in the Glossary section.

- Project Manager
- Project Sponsor
- Business Analyst
- Technical Lead

IDENTIFY THE PROJECT SPONSOR

If a Project Sponsor has not been identified, the Project Manager must work with Customer management to identify and formally appoint someone to that position.

Because the Project Sponsor will champion the project within the organization, secure spending authority and resources, and provide support to the Project Manager, it is imperative that he/she be identified as early in the project management lifecycle as possible. Building the relationship between the Project Manager and the Project Sponsor is critical to project success.

IDENTIFY PROJECT TEAM

At a minimum the manager for the project and certain individuals who can provide support in preparing for the project should be identified. In selecting the Project Team, definition of the skills required to perform current tasks as well as skills for future project tasks is needed. Immediate project needs should be met first. After Project Team members have been identified, the Project Manager should provide them with a project orientation and review with individual team members their current and future roles on the project. This establishes a baseline understanding of team members' project responsibilities, which will be useful for conducting performance reviews later in the project.

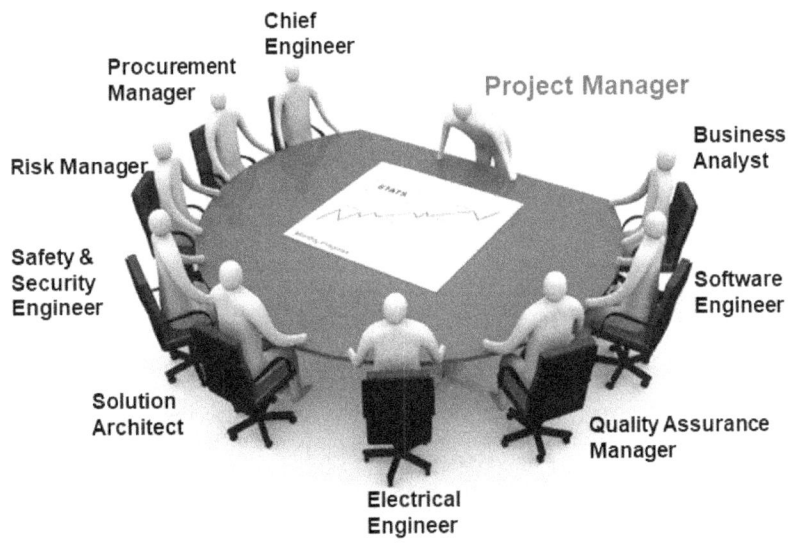

REVIEW HISTORICAL DATA

Development of the Project Charter will require review of documentation compiled or presented during Project Origination. Materials and information reviewed may include: the strategic plan, a formal document produced by the Customer that outlines the business goals and direction over a designated number of years; the Project Proposal, including the initial Business Case, which describes the project objectives and how they support the Customer's strategic business direction; project selection criteria, defining the parameters used in determining whether or not to undertake a project and identifying its business justification and measurements of its success; and information from a previous project similar in size, scope and objectives.

DEVELOPING THE PROJECT CHARTER

The purpose of developing the Project Charter is to document critical success factors; define and secure commitment for the resources required to complete System Initiation. The charter also documents the project's mission, history, and background, describes the business problem the project is intended to resolve, and lists the benefits to be realized by the Customer as a result of implementing the product or service. To write an effective, comprehensive charter, the Project Manager must work with the Project Sponsor and any appropriate subject matter experts and Stakeholders.

 **Develop Project Charter**

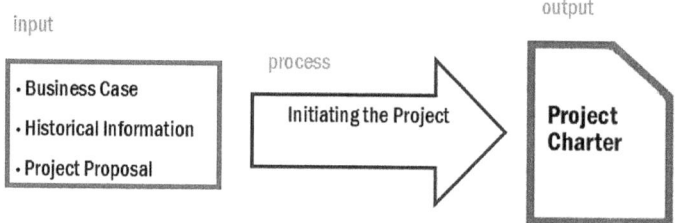

Develop Project Charter is the task of developing a document that formally authorizes the existence of a project. It provides the project manager with the authority to assign resources to project activities.

The Project Charter should summarize the scope, schedule, budget, quality objectives, deliverables, and milestones of the project. Any risks or assumptions should be documented in the Project Charter. Assumptions may include things that must go right, such as a particular team member being available for the project, or specific criteria used in developing the Project Management plan estimates. It should serve as an important communication tool that provides a consolidated source of information about the project that can be referenced throughout the project life cycle. The Project Charter should not only identify the project sponsor, project manager, and project team, but also when and how they will be involved throughout the project life cycle.

 ## Develop Project Charter

Develop Project Charter is the task of developing a document that formally authorizes the existence of a project. It provides the project manager with the authority to assign resources to project activities.

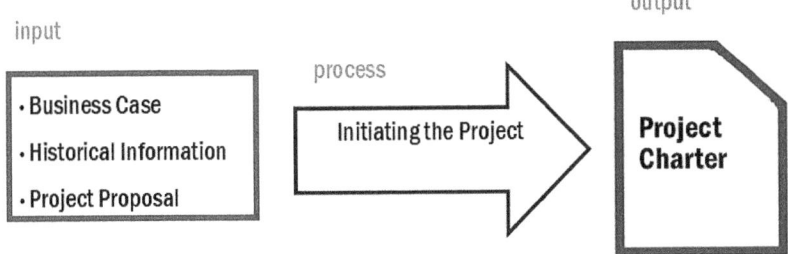

EXAMINING THE PROJECT CHARTER

The Project Charter is an output of the System Initiation processes and serves as an input to System Requirements phase. The Project Charter, as you know by now, authorizes the project. Projects do not exist without a Project Charter. In some instances, however, a contract can serve as the Project Charter. As a quick review, here are some exam essentials you should know about the Project Charter:

- The Project Charter names the project and provides a description of the product.
- The Project Charter names the project manager and assigns the project manager a level of authority for managing resources, finances, and decisions on the project.

- The Project Charter details the Business Case of the project. The Business Case identifies the business need behind the project, and establishes why the project has been created.
- The Project Charter provides detailed product description. This is a description of the desired future state the project will create.
- The Project Charter is signed and approved by a member of management that has the proper authority to ascertain the needed resources and charge the project manager with the management duties. The person signing the charter is high enough in the organization to be considered 'over' the project team members and functional managers.
- The Project Charter should be written so as not to require change as the project progresses.

ESTABLISH THE PROJECT REPOSITORY

Maintaining information about the project in an organized fashion facilitates new team member transitions and creates a central point of reference for those developing project definition documents. Most importantly, it provides an audit trail documenting the history and evolution of the project. All relevant project-related material, documents produced, decisions made, issues raised and correspondence exchanged must be captured for future reference and historical tracking.

By the end of the project, a project repository may include the following materials:

- Project Proposal and supporting documentation, including the Business Case
- Project description/definition documents such as the Project Charter and the Project Management plan

- Any working documents or informal documents defining Cost, Scope, Schedule and Quality of the project
- Project Schedules (baseline and current)
- Project financials
- Project Scope changes and requests log
- Project Status Reports
- Team member Progress Reports and timesheets
- Issue log and details (open and resolved)
- Project acceptance log by deliverable
- Risk identification/model documentation
- Audit results
- Correspondence, including any pivotal or decision-making
- Meeting notes, results, and/or actions

Project Repository

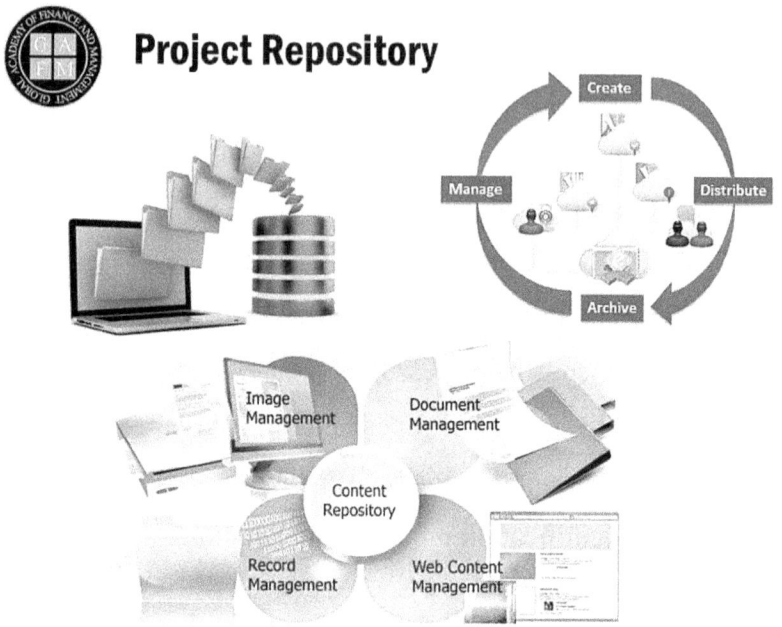

DEFINE SCOPE

The written scope statement is a document that serves as input to future System Design efforts. The scope statement should include:

- the business needs the project will address
- what the project will accomplish, how it will be accomplished and by whom
- what the end result of the project will be (e.g., a product, service, other).
- a list of project deliverables, which, when produced and accepted, indicate project completion.

Also included is a list of those deliverables that are not in scope for the project. The Project Manager must be specific about what is in scope and what is not in scope, as the weaker the boundaries between the two, the more difficult it will be to effect the change control process if required later in the project. Also, the details regarding what is in and what is out of scope are critical input to the creation of a detailed Project Schedule. The Project Charter, including the project outcome description, provides necessary information for defining the Project Scope relative to the business need and benefit for the organization undertaking the project.

Project Scope Statement is the basis for confirming a common understanding of the project outcomes and making future decisions regarding the project.

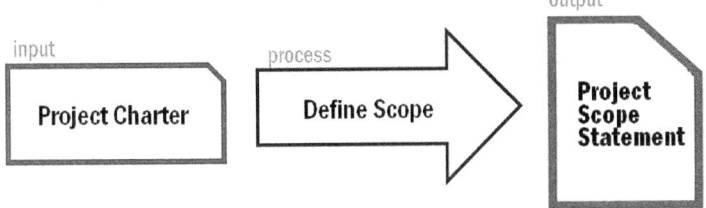

PRELIMINARY SCOPE STATEMENT

The preliminary scope statement which is an output of System Initiation, is the guide for all future project decisions. It is the key document to provide understanding of the project purpose. The scope statement provides justification for the project existence, lists the high-level deliverables, and quantifies the project objectives. The scope statement is a powerful document that the project manager and the project team will use as a point of reference for potential changes, added work, and any project decisions.

The scope statement includes or references the following:

- **Project justification**: Identifies the business needs of the project. It answers why the project has been authorized. This is important since it provides guidance should the project undergo cuts and trade-offs of deliverables.

- **Project's product**: The scope statement reiterates the details of the project product.

- **Project deliverables**: The high-level deliverables of the project should be identified. These deliverables, when predefined metrics are met, signal that the project scope has been completed. When appropriate, the scope statement should also list what deliverables are excluded from the project deliverables. For example, a project to create a new food product may state that it is not including the packaging of the food product as part of the project. Items and features not listed as part of the project deliverables should be assumed to be excluded.

- **Project objectives**: Project objectives are specific conditions that determine the success of a project. Conditions are typically cost, schedule, and quality metrics. Vague metrics, such as customer satisfaction, increase risk for the project, as the metric 'customer satisfaction' is subjective and not quantified.

HIGH-LEVEL PROJECT SCHEDULE

A high-level project schedule is a calendar-based representation of work that will be accomplished during a project. Developing a schedule means determining the start and end dates for all tasks required to produce the project's product, and the project management deliverables. At this early stage in the project management lifecycle, information required to complete a project schedule is known only at an overview level, often based solely upon the expert judgment of the Project Manager or other individuals with experience managing projects with similar lifecycles. Even at a high-level, this information still provides insight into preparing the first draft of a project schedule. The activities documented in the schedule at this early stage will be further broken-down during System Design, when the schedule will be refined to include the specific individuals assigned and the amount of time required to complete the work. Using Excel, a Project Manager can develop a project schedule worksheet to develop the high-level Project Schedule. The best approach is to use a Work Breakdown Structure (WBS) to develop the high-level project schedule.

Develop High Level Project Schedule

Developing a project schedule means determining the start and end dates for all tasks required to produce the project's product, and the project management deliverables.

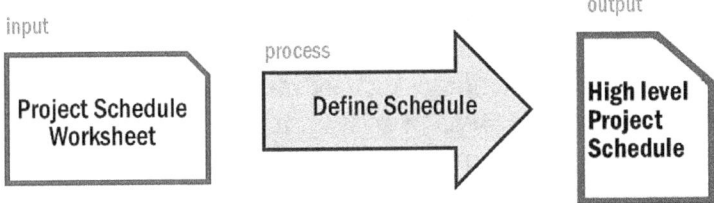

At this stage the effort and time required to complete the work cannot be determined. The activities documented in the schedule at this early stage will be further broken down during Project Planning, when the schedule will be refined to include the specific individuals assigned and the amount of time required to complete the work. We shall use a Project Schedule Worksheet to create the high-level project schedule.

QUALITY REQUIREMENTS

If the Customer has established quality standards, the Project Manager can reference the document containing the quality standards the organization already has in place. In most cases, however, this document does not exist, or the quality standards are not in place.

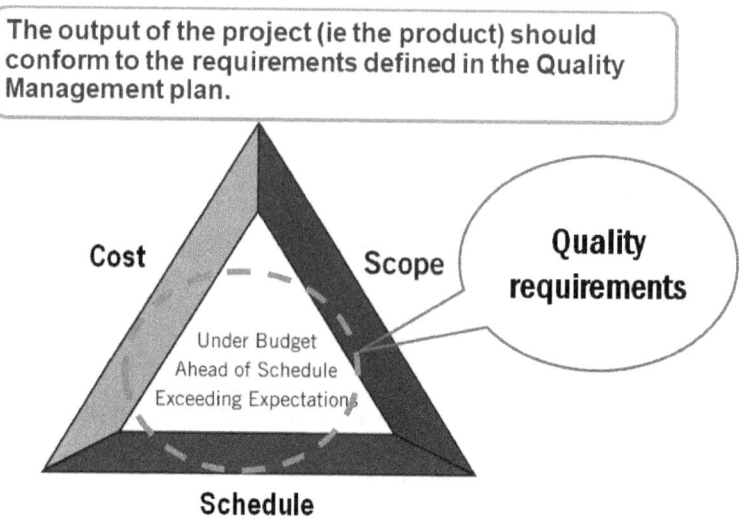

The Project Manager and Customer must identify and document standards for each project deliverable during System Initiation. If quality standards are not identified and documented, the Project Manager will have no way to determine if deliverables are being produced to an acceptable quality level. The Project Scope statement documents what the outcome of the project will be and will help determine the appropriate quality standards to use.

PRELIMINARY PROJECT BUDGET

The Project Manager should use manual or automated tools to generate a Preliminary Project Budget. The budgeting tools may be simple spreadsheets or complex mathematical modelling tools. The Project Manager calculates the preliminary budget that will be required to complete project activities. All aspects of the project, including the cost of human resources, equipment, travel, materials and supplies, should be incorporated.

BUDGET INFORMATION

Phase	Process/Task	Labor Cost	Material Cost	Travel Cost	Other Cost	Total Cost	Planned Date of Expenditure

- The Phase, Process, and Task names come from the High-Level Schedule.
- The Labor Cost is the cost of human resources required to perform the Task.
- The Material Cost is the cost for equipment and supplies including services.
- The Travel Cost is any predicted cost that will be incurred if travel is required.
- Enter miscellaneous costs eg. person, expenses, and travel costs under Other Costs.
- Total the costs for each activity and enter the total under Total Cost.
- Then enter the Planned Date the expenditure will be incurred.

At this point information will be presented at a summary level to be refined during System Design usually after completion of System Requirements and as more detailed information becomes known. The Project Manager must also have a general understanding of the cost of both the human resources and the equipment and materials required to perform the work. The method by which staff and products will be acquired for the project will directly affect the budgeting process. A number of constraints, financial, political, and organizational, may dictate the methods by which required individuals, equipment, and materials are acquired. The Project Manager needs to be aware of existing resource acquisition policies, guidelines, and procedures.

TYPES OF COST

- **Sunk Costs:** A historical or expended cost. Since the cost has been expended, we no longer have control over the cost. Sunk costs are not included when considering alternative courses of action.

- **Fixed Costs**: Nonrecurring costs that do not change based on the number of units, like expenses related to equipment required to complete a project.
- **Variable Costs**: Costs that rise directly with the size of the project, like expenses related to consumable materials used to accomplish the project.
- **Indirect Costs**: Costs that are part of the overall organization's cost of doing business and are shared among all the current projects. These include salaries of corporate executives, administrative expenses, and any cost that would be considered part of project overhead expenses.
- **Opportunity Costs:** The cost of choosing one alternative and, therefore, giving up the potential benefits of another alternative.
- **Direct Costs:** Costs incurred directly by a specific project. These include cost for materials associated with the project, salary of the project staff, expenses associated with subcontractors.

RISK IDENTIFICATION

The Project Manager solicits input from the Project Team, Project Sponsor, and from Customer Representatives, who try to anticipate any possible events, obstacles, or issues that may produce unplanned outcomes during the course of the project. Risks to both internal and external aspects of the project should be assessed. Internal risks are events that the Project Team can directly control, while external risks happen outside the direct influence of the Project Team.

The project should be analyzed for risk in areas such as:

- culture of the Customer
- anticipated impact on the Customer of the resulting product or service

- the level to which the end result is defined (the more complete the definition, the lower the possibility of risk)
- technology used on the project (proven vs. new)
- relationships among team members
- impact on work units

Historical information can be extremely helpful in determining potential project risks. Data and documentation from previous projects, or interviews with team members or other subject matter experts from past projects provide excellent insight into potential risk areas and ways to avoid or mitigate them.

Risk is at its peak at the early stage of the project

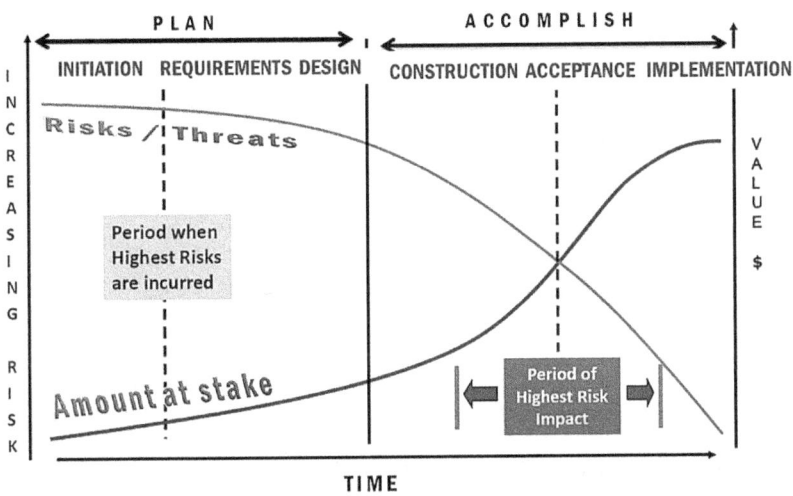

The Project Manager documents identified risks to inform the risk identification and assessment process. Risk identification lists are typically organized by source of risk to help the Project Manager organize and record ideas. These lists may be generic or industry-specific. The Project Manager may even decide to create risk identification lists specifically geared toward the current project. At this point, the Project Team is simply identifying and listing risks. At this stage the identified risks are listed in a document called the Initial Risk Register.

CATEGORIES OF RISK

As risks are identified within the project, they should be categorized. Risk categories should be identified before risk identification begins and should include common risks that are typical in the industry where the project is occurring. Risk categories help organize, rank, and isolate risks within the project. There are four major categories of risks:

- **Technical, quality, or performance risks**

Technical risks are associated with new, unproven, or complex technology being used on the project. Changes to the technology during the project implementation can also be a risk. Quality risks are the levels set for expectations of impractical quality and performance. Changes to industry standards during the project can also be lumped into this category of risks.

- **Project management risks**

These risks deal with faults in the management of the project: unsuccessful allocation of time, resources, and scheduling; unacceptable work results (low-quality work); and lousy project management as a whole.

- **Organizational risks**

The Customer can contribute to the project risks through unreasonable cost, time, and scope expectations; poor project prioritization; inadequate funding or the disruption of funding; and the competition with other projects for internal resources.

- **External risks**

These risks are outside of the project but directly affect it: legal issues, labor issues, a shift in project priorities, and weather.

Force majeure risks can be scary and usually call for disaster recovery rather than project management. These are risks caused by earthquakes, tornados, floods, civil unrest, and other disasters.

Return on Investment

The outcome/benefits will only be realized after the project is completed.

Risks need to be managed and controlled to realize project profitability.

HISTORICAL INFORMATION

Historical information is always an excellent source of information for risk identification. If the Customer has done similar projects in the past, the historical information should be able to shed light on the risks identified early in the project, as well as risks identified throughout the project, and provide information in the final project reports. In addition to the documentation, stakeholders of the original project may have information to offer based on their experience within the project.

REVIEWING PROJECT DOCUMENTS

One of the first steps the project team should take is to review the project documentation. The Project Management plan, scope, and other project files should be reviewed. Constraints and assumptions should be reviewed, considered, and analyzed for risks. This structure review takes a very broad look at the Project Management plan, the scope, and the activities defined within the project.

BRAINSTORMING THE PROJECT

Brainstorming is likely the most common approach to risk identification. It is usually completed together as a project team to identify the risks within the project. The risks are identified in broad terms and posted, and then the risks characteristics are detailed. The identified risks are categorized and will pass through qualitative and quantitative risk analysis later. A multidisciplinary team, hosted by a project facilitator, can also complete brainstorming.

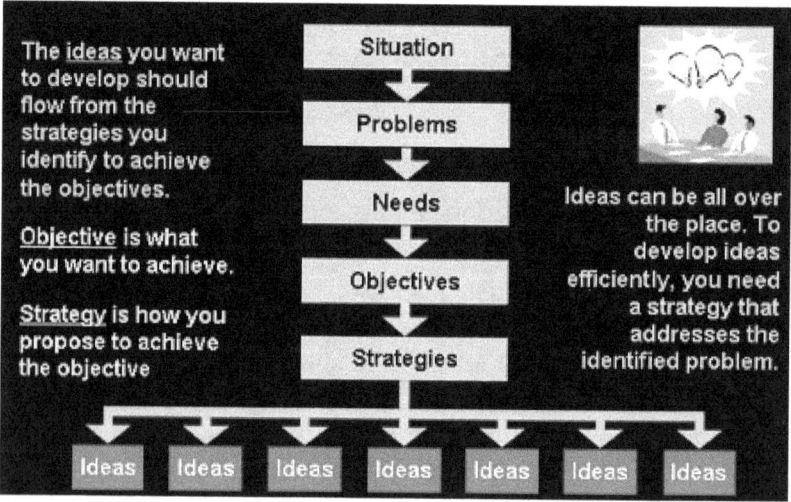

This approach can include subject matter experts, project team members, customers, and other stakeholders to contribute to the risk identification process.

USING THE DELPHI TECHNIQUE

The Delphi Technique is an anonymous method to query experts about foreseeable risks within a project, phase, or component of a project. The results of the survey are analyzed by a third party, organized, and then circulated to the experts. There can be several rounds of anonymous discussion with the Delphi Technique without fear of backlash or offending other participants in the process.

Identify Stakeholders

In addition to compiling these work products, developing the initial Project Management plan involves identifying the Stakeholders that will be involved in the project and establishing and documenting a plan for project communications. The Project Manager defines the organization of the Project Team and outlines Stakeholders' roles and responsibilities. All Stakeholders who will be involved in some capacity on the project should be identified.

Develop Communications Management Plan

The Communications Management plan is a document describing the means by which project communications will occur. The Project Manager must receive input from Project Team members and Stakeholders about their information and communications requirements, determine the best and most cost-effective way in which the requirements can be met, and record the information in a formal, approved document.

 # Project Communications

Communications Management is involved with the processes required to ensure timely and appropriate generation, collection, distribution, storage, retrieval, and ultimate disposition of project information.

Similarly, the Project Manager must provide details to the team and the Stakeholders regarding the communications he/she expects to receive, and document these requirements in the plan.

- How often and how quickly information needs to be disseminated.
- By what means the Project Manager and Stakeholders prefer to receive information (via phone, email, paper).
- The communication mechanism currently used in the organization, and how it might be leveraged or improved.
- The effectiveness of communications in past projects and whether specific improvements were recommended.

Communications Schedule

Event	Purpose	Frequency
Project team meetings	Clearly identify the expected business benefits	Weekly
Quality review meetings	To ensure that quality issues are identified early.	Monthly
Phase review meetings	To control the progress of the project through each phase.	Weekly
Change approval meetings	To provide a formal process for the approval of project changes	Weekly
Customer Acceptance meetings	To provide a controlled process for the acceptance of deliverables.	deliverable completion
Project Update meetings	To keep all key project stakeholders informed of the status of the project.	Weekly

Based on stakeholder analysis, the project manager and the project team can determine what communications are needed. There is no advantage to supplying stakeholders with information that is not needed or desired. Time spent creating and delivering unneeded information is a waste of resources. A Communications Management plan can organize and document the process, types, and expectations of communications. It provides:

- A system to gather, organize, store, and disseminate appropriate information to the appropriate people. The system includes procedures for correcting and updating incorrect information that may have been distributed.
- Details on how needed information flows through the project to the correct individuals. The communication structure documents where the information will originate, to whom the information will be sent, and in what modality the information is acceptable.

- Specifics on how the information to be distributed should be organized, the level of expected detail for the types of communication, and the terminology expected within the communications.
- Schedules of when the various types of communication should occur. Some communication, such as status meetings, should happen on a regular schedule; other communications may be prompted by conditions within the project.
- Methods to retrieve information as needed.
- Instructions on how the Communications Management plan can be updated as the project progresses.

PRELIMINARY PROJECT MANAGEMENT PLAN

The Project Management plan is a collection of information used to describe the environment that will govern the project. The work products previously produced during System Initiation become part of the Preliminary Project Management plan. In addition to compiling these work products, developing the Preliminary Project Management plan involves identifying the Stakeholders that will be involved in the project and establishing and documenting a plan for project communications. The Preliminary Project Management plan is an evolving set of documents where new information will continue to be added and existing information will be revised during System Design.

All work products and deliverables from System Initiation processes will be compiled for the Preliminary Project Management plan. At this point in the project management lifecycle, the Preliminary Project Management plan will consist of the following information:

- Project Charter
- Cost, Scope, Schedule, Quality
- List of Risks

- Description of Stakeholder Involvement
- Communications Plan

This information will be refined and supplemented in later project phases as the Project Manager and team become more knowledgeable about the project and its definition. The Preliminary Project Management plan is not a static document; it requires iterative refinement.

Preliminary Project Management plan is the key deliverable produced during System Initiation. The initial plan will be refined iteratively throughout the entire project management lifecycle and will serve as the main guide to follow during System Construction and System Acceptance. The Preliminary Project Management plan incorporates the deliverables above and is used to:

- Document System Design assumptions
- Document System Design decisions regarding alternatives chosen
- Facilitate communication among internal and external Stakeholders
- Define key management reviews as to content, extent and timing
- Provide a baseline for progress measurement and project control

Chapter 3 : SYSTEM REQUIREMENTS

REQUIREMENTS GATHERING TECHNIQUES

Identifying requirements

This involves stating requirements in simple sentences and providing them as a set. Business needs or requirements are the essential activities of an enterprise. They are derived from business goals (the objectives of the enterprise). Business scenarios may be used as a technique for understanding business requirements. A key factor in the success of a system is the extent to which it supports the business requirements and facilitates an organization in achieving them.

Clarifying and restating the requirements

This is done to ensure that they describe the customer's real needs and are in a form that can be understood and used by developers of the system.

Analyzing the requirements

This is done to ensure that they are well defined and that they conform to the criteria of a good requirement.

Defining the requirements

Defining the requirements in a way that means the same thing to all of the stakeholders. Note that each stakeholder group may have a significantly different perspective of the system and the system's requirements. Sometimes this requires investing significant time learning a special vocabulary or project lexicon. Often it requires spending considerable time and effort to achieve a common understanding.

Specifying the requirements

This requires including all of the precise detail of each requirement so that it can be included in a specification document or other documentation, depending on the size of the project.

Prioritizing the requirements

All requirements are not of equal importance to the customers and users of the planned system. Some are critical, some of relatively high priority, some of normal or average priority, and some even of lower priority. It is important to prioritize all of the requirements because there is never enough time or money to do everything we'd like to do in our developed systems. Prioritizing the requirements provides the opportunity to address the highest priority first and possibly release a version of a product that addresses lower-priority needs. Prioritizing helps ensure that an appropriate amount of investment is made in meeting various customer needs.

Deriving requirements

There are some requirements that come about because of the design of a system, but do not provide a direct benefit to the end user. A requirement for disc storage might result from the need to store a lot of data, for example.

Partitioning requirements

We categorize requirements as those that can be met by hardware, software, training, and documentation, for example. Often this process turns out to be more complex than we anticipate when some requirements are satisfied by more than one category.

Allocating requirements

We allocate requirements to different subsystems and components of the system. The allocations may not always be satisfied by just one subsystem or component.

Tracking requirements

We need the capability to trace or track where in the system each requirement is satisfied, so that we can verify that each requirement is being addressed. This is most often accomplished through use of an automated requirements tool.

Managing requirements

We need to be able to add, delete, and modify requirements during all of the phases of system design, development, integration, testing, deployment, and operation. The requirements repository consists of a set of artifacts and databases.

Testing and verifying requirements

This are the process of checking requirements, designs, code, test plans, and system products to ensure that the requirements are met.

Validating requirements

This is the process for confirming that the real requirements are implemented in the delivered system. The order of validation of requirements should be prioritized since there is a limited amount of funding available.

TYPES OF REQUIREMENTS

It's important for the RA or requirements engineer to settle on definitions of the types of requirements that he will use consistently. He should advocate consistent meanings for these types on his project and in his organization. Much confusion can be avoided by agreeing on a set of definitions and by not using certain terms. In this chapter, we'll review several types of requirements and suggest definitions for them. We'll suggest why some terms shouldn't be used and provide other guidelines. One important reason for agreeing on the definitions of the types of requirements is to avoid lengthy and heated debates about terminology while we are working together. Establish a project glossary that everyone can live with (even if some definitions are not everyone's favorites) and utilize it in your work.

A requirement is a statement that identifies a capability, characteristic, or quality factor of a system in order for it to have value and utility for a user. A requirement is well-defined and more specific than a need, which is a capability desired by a user or customer to solve a problem or achieve an objective.

The requirements types that are noted are production process requirements (e.g., the physical facilities needed), requirements of the products to be provided by the system or software, the requirements of the processes utilized to produce the products (e.g., the testing process), and operational and logistics support requirements (e.g., equipment, training, and procedures). All of these requirements must be identified before work on the detailed system design is started. While the product engineers are developing specifications for the product elements, the manufacturing engineers must define the manufacturing requirements, the logistics engineers the logistics requirements, and the verification engineers the qualification requirements. While doing so, these engineers must communicate among themselves and jointly resolve the best aggregate expression of the requirements from the product and process perspective.

BUSINESS REQUIREMENTS

Business requirements are the reason for developing systems and software in the first place. Business requirements are the essential activities of an enterprise. Business requirements are derived from business goals (the objectives of the enterprise or organization). Business scenarios may be used as a technique for understanding business requirements. A key factor in the success of a system is the extent to which the system supports the business requirements and facilitates an organization in achieving them. If our systems and software do not support the business requirements effectively and efficiently, they have no reason to be.

HIGH-LEVEL OR SYSTEM-LEVEL REQUIREMENTS

To enable comprehending a needed system, we refer to the high-level or system-level requirements. This term relates to those requirements that are foremost in importance, capture the vision of the customer, enable defining the scope of the system, and allow estimating the cost and schedule required to build the system. (Some system architects believe that the requirements specification should contain every performance requirement.) It's recommended that a workable number of requirements (on the order of 50 to 200) system-level requirements be identified for a large system.

FUNCTIONAL REQUIREMENTS

Functional requirements are an important category of the real requirements. Functional requirements describe what the system or software must do. A function is a useful capability provided by one or more components of a system. Functional requirements are sometimes called behavioral or operational requirements because they specify the inputs to the system, the outputs (responses) from the system, and behavioral relationships between them. The document used to communicate the requirements to customers, system, and software engineers is referred to as a functional document (FD) or specification. This refers to a comprehensive collection of the characteristics of a system and the capabilities it will make available to the users. It provides a detailed analysis of the data the system will be expected to manipulate. It may include a detailed definition of the user interfaces of the system.

DERIVED REQUIREMENTS

A derived requirement is one that is further refined from a higher-level requirement or a requirement that results from choosing a specific implementation or system element. In a sense, all requirements are derived from the system need; thus, the derived distinction tends to have little significance. However, many systems engineers distinguish between externally identified requirements and requirements that are derived under the control of the engineer.

DESIGN REQUIREMENTS AND DESIGN CONSTRAINTS

For most system development efforts, design requirements/constraints appear right at the beginning of the system formulation. Here are examples of why it's difficult to separate requirements engineering from design activities:

- New systems are often installed in environments that already have other systems. The other systems usually constrain the design of the new system. For example, a requirement (design constraint) may be that the system to be developed must obtain its information from an existing database. The database has already been designed and parts of its specification will usually be included in the requirements document.
- For large systems, some architectural design is often necessary to identify subsystems and relationships.

Identifying subsystems means that the requirements engineering process for each subsystem can go on in parallel.

- For reasons of budget, schedule, or quality, an organization may wish to reuse some or all existing software systems in the implementation of a new system. This constrains both the system requirements and the design.
- If a system has to be approved by an external regulator (e.g., systems in civil aircraft), it may be necessary to use standard certified design that has been tested in other systems.

Environmental Requirements

These are requirements that result from the physical setting and social and cultural conditions of the system development effort and the setting in which the system or software will be used.

System, Subsystem, and Component Requirements

This refers to requirements associated with different levels of the system. The system is the highest level and is divided into subsystems; the subsystems are made up of components, such as hardware, software, training, and documentation.

Key Requirements

The term key requirements are sometimes used to refer to requirements that are important in order to understand a system's essential capabilities or functions. 4 It is appropriate to analyze requirements in terms of their benefit-to-cost ratio, risk, or the estimated time and effort needed to address them, so that we can have informal discussions within the joint team to negotiate the requirements to be included. However, I suggest avoiding use of this term, because it's unclear.

GATHERING REQUIREMENTS

The need to gather requirements is initiated by a request from an internal or external customer. Requests can come in many forms, including a request for proposals, an SOW, or an informal or formal inquiry describing a capability that is needed. The request initiates a set of requirements-gathering activities. It's vital for the RA to have a thorough understanding of these activities and to gain experience in performing related tasks.

Requirements gathering

- Requirements gathering, when properly facilitated, establishes a forum for everyone to be heard, for issues to be worked through, and for resolutions to be defined that meet the needs of all parties.
- Through this forum, multiple opinions may enhance the team's understanding of how certain processes are currently being performed, better defining how they should be structured within the context of the new application.
- This approach may also result in negotiations of functionality.
- There may need to be some trade-offs, and as a result processes may be reexamined and redefined.
- As the sessions progress, the Project Team must constantly assess and analyze the requirements.

A lot of time and effort is wasted in the project startup phase and in performing requirements-gathering activities. There are several reasons for this:

- The project is just getting organized and things are confusing.
- There is no road map or checklist of startup activities.
- Not all staff are present; some are still being recruited.
- There isn't much pressure to meet the schedule yet.

- The customer and users are also trying to get organized and get started.

- The staff who will be working on end-product development may not fully understand the customer's objectives and, consequently, may not be able to appreciate the customer's expectations.

- An effective proven procedure for the requirements gathering steps is not available or used.

The purpose of system requirements is to obtain a thorough and detailed understanding of the business need as defined in the project conceptual phase and captured in the Business Case, and to break it down into discrete requirements, which are then clearly defined, reviewed and agreed upon with the Customer Decision-Makers. The project conceptual phase is not part of the SDLC, it is the phase where the project feasibility study was conducted which resulted in the production of the project Business Case. During System Requirements phase, the framework for the application is developed, providing the foundation for all future design and development efforts.

System Requirements can be a challenging phase because all of the major Customers and their interests are brought into the process of determining requirements. The quality of the final product is highly dependent on the effectiveness of the requirements analysis process. Since the requirements form the basis for all future work on the project, from design and development to testing and documentation, it is of the utmost importance that the Project Team create a complete and accurate representation of all requirements that the system must accommodate. Accurately identified requirements result from effective communication and collaboration among all members of the Project Team, that provide the best chance of creating a system that fully satisfies the needs of the Customers.

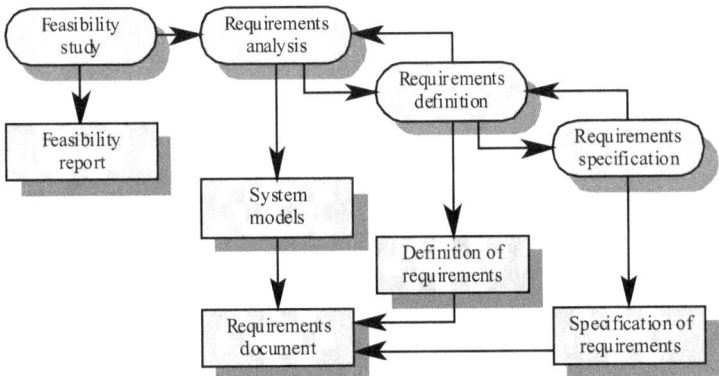

The primary goal of this phase is to create a detailed Functional Specification defining the full set of system capabilities to be implemented, along with accompanying data and process models illustrating the information to be managed and the processes to be supported by the new system. The Functional Specification will evolve throughout the SDLC phases as detailed business requirements are captured, and as supporting process and data models are created, ensuring that the eventual solution provides the Customers with the functionality they need to meet their stated business objectives.

THE PEOPLE

The following roles are involved in carrying out the processes of this phase.

- Project Manager
- Project Sponsor
- Facilitator
- Business Analyst
- Database Administrator

- Data Process Modeler
- Technical Architect
- Quality Assurance Analyst
- Technical Support
- Information Security
- Customer Decision-Maker
- Customer Representative
- Consumer
- Customer
- Stakeholders

MANAGING PROJECT TEAM

In order to successfully meet the needs of a project, it is important to have a high-performing Project Team made up of individuals who are both technically skilled and motivated to contribute to the project's outcome. One of the many responsibilities of a Project Manager is to enhance the ability of each Project Team member to contribute to the project, while also fostering individual growth and accomplishment. At the same time, each individual must be encouraged to share ideas and work with others toward a common goal. The Project Manager, then, must be a leader, communicator, negotiator, influencer, and problem solver! The level of skills and competencies to successfully fill these roles helps distinguish good Project Managers from great ones.

During System Construction, the Project Manager must review the contents of the Training Plan to be sure they are still applicable to the project. If additional training is necessary, it should be added to the plan. If it is determined that planned training is no longer necessary, it must be removed from the plan. If new team members have joined the project since the Training Plan was established, the Project Manager must evaluate the skill level of the new members to determine if additional training is needed. In all cases, training tasks must be added to or removed from both the Training Plan and the Project Schedule, since they will affect the end date of the project.

Some personnel may be transferred to different assignments or leave their employers, new individuals may be added to a Project Team or Customer organization, or the nature of the project may change, forcing a change in project responsibilities or reporting structure. A successful Project Manager has a plan in place to minimize the effect these types of changes may have on the outcome of the project or the morale of the Project Team. At a minimum, this plan should describe what to do when there are changes to the Project Team, but it should also discuss the actions to take if the Customers change. The process may be formal or very informal, depending on the size and needs of the project. In all cases, changes to the Project Team or Customer will most likely require updates to the Project Schedule.

INITIATE SYSTEM REQUIREMENTS

The purpose of Initiate System Requirements is to position the Project Team and their working environment to ensure successful completion of system requirements tasks. This is the point at which the Project Team prepares to capture the detailed functional, technical, operational, and transitional requirements of the system.

In preparing for this phase, the Project Manager must focus on the Project Team and the environment in which the team will work. With each new project phase comes the need for new skills, experience, and, potentially, new Project Team members. The team needed during this phase must possess analytical skills that allow them to continually drive to deeper levels of requirements definition. Experience in effective interviewing, facilitation, various modelling techniques, requirements gathering, and gap analysis will be extremely beneficial.

In reviewing the validated solution all team members must share a clear and common understanding of the scope of this phase of the project, the Project Schedule, the deliverables to be produced, and their responsibilities relating to the creation of these deliverables.

Regardless of the size of the development effort being undertaken, System Requirements phase may place the greatest demand upon Customers in terms of resources and the extent of their required participation. During the preparation for this phase, the Project Manager should continue to manage the Customer's expectations surrounding this participation. Less involvement typically leads to a less acceptable finished product. In addition, many individuals earmarked to participate in the requirements gathering sessions may not have been privy to earlier project scope setting sessions. This can lead to the possible perception of these upcoming sessions as opportunities to identify or request functionality and features that are beyond the original intent of the project. Since management of scope creep is an essential role of the Project Manager, this may be an appropriate time to review the established change management processes with the Customer.

At the start of the System Requirements phase, it is the Project Manager's responsibility to ensure that the environment in which the Project Team will work is properly established. Beyond the obvious need to ensure that team members have adequate equipment to perform their duties, there are additional elements of the environment that should not be overlooked.

The project repository, a secure area for maintaining work products and deliverables that was established during System Initiation, continues to evolve over subsequent phases of the project. Although the establishment of the repository itself is important, it is equally necessary to define the mechanisms and processes to be followed for creating and maintaining all System Requirements phase related materials.

COLLECT BUSINESS REQUIREMENTS

While this process specifically addresses the capturing of Business Requirements for the new system, the reality is that it may be necessary, and is often beneficial, for the Project Team to determine these requirements while simultaneously defining the supporting process and data models. By conducting these three processes (Collect Business Requirements, Define Process Model, and Define Logical Data Model) concurrently, as opposed to sequentially, the team can develop the process and data models as information and requirements are defined, and can update these models as a result of gathering new or changed information.

Because the three processes are performed not only concurrently, but also often iteratively, it is important for the Project Team to tightly manage the documentation for each process so that requirements are not lost, misunderstood or overlooked. The Project Manager may need to utilize techniques and/or tools to help document requirements and ensure that they are not missed. The Glossary contains a brief description of some of the techniques available to the Project Manager; examples include storyboarding, interviews, joint application design sessions (JAD), Unified Modelling Language (UML), prototyping, data flow diagramming, process modelling, and entity-relationship diagramming.

Determining Business Requirements requires eliciting, analyzing, specifying, prioritizing, verifying and negotiating business functions that the system must deliver and support. During this process it is important to have all of the Stakeholders involved. Since this is the process in which all business and processing requirements are determined and agreed to, it is critical that all parties understand the ramifications of including or excluding requirements from scope. This is an opportunity to work out business process issues as a group, in order to reach optimal performance and efficiency within an organization or even across organizations or functional areas. Decisions made will impact remaining phases, so all parties involved in the project lifecycle should be heard, and all areas of concern or question should be thoroughly addressed. Reaching consensus and agreement on the final deliverable from this phase will help to ensure that everyone gets the product to which they agreed.

1. **Functional Requirements** that define those features of the system requirements which will specifically satisfy a Consumer need, or with which the Consumer will directly interact.
2. **Technical Requirements** that define the technical constraints or requirements under which the system must perform.
3. **Operational Requirements** that define those "behind the scenes" requirements that are needed to keep the system operational over time.
4. **Transitional Requirements** that define those aspects of the system that requirements must be addressed in order for the system to be successfully implemented in the production environment, and to relegate support responsibilities to the Customer.

 # Business Requirements document

A document containing detailed requirements for the product. These requirements define the functional, technical, operational, and transitional capabilities, restrictions, and features that must be provided.

DEFINE PROCESS MODEL

The purpose of the Define Process Model is to create a pictorial representation of the functions and operations (i.e., the processes) that will eventually be performed by the system being developed.

The second of the three concurrent processes within System Requirements phase, Define the Process Model may begin at any time after the Project Team has started collecting specific business requirements. The resulting Process Model of the system, also often referred to as the "To Be" model, illustrates the system processes as they are envisioned for the new system. Over time, this pictorial top-down representation of the major business processes will be decomposed into manageable functions and sub-functions until no further breakdown is possible. When combined with the detailed set of Business Requirements and the supporting Logical Data Model, this Process Model should completely address not only the full list of business needs to be satisfied by the new system, but also the vision for how the new system will provide and support this functionality.

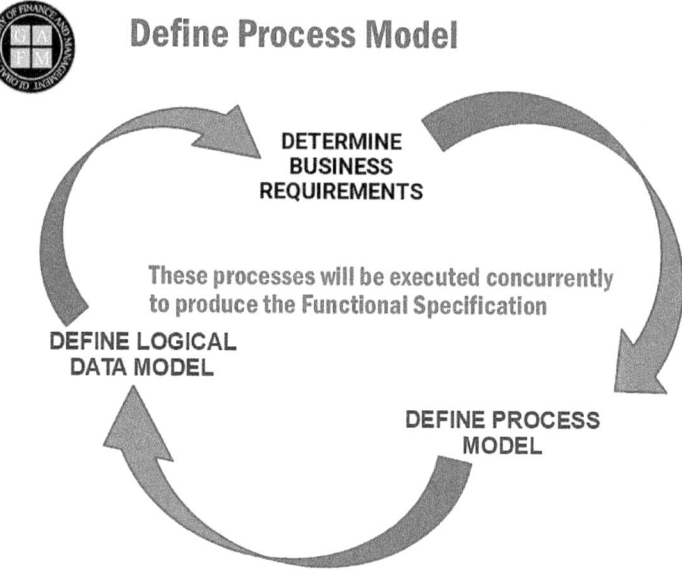

Define Process Model

During the Determine Business Requirements process, a picture of the current business processes and practices will begin to evolve. This can be a useful tool in confirming that all current processes have been identified, and can be used by the Project Team as a means of ensuring that their Process Model has not neglected any existing functionality. There is a risk, however, that too much focus on current business processes may cause Customers to take a myopic view of their true business needs, ultimately defining a system that provides little value over the system that is already in place.

The Project Manager must ensure that the Stakeholders and Customers periodically validate the Process Model as it is being developed. It is important that they understand that the Process Model is a representation of the proposed business solution, an attempt to meet everyone's needs. As part of validating the final Process Model deliverable with the Customer, it may be beneficial to conduct walk-throughs to map the defined business requirements to the diagrammed Process Model. A walk-through helps to identify any requirements missed by both the Project Team and the Customer, and helps to further validate that the requirements and processes are accurately decomposed.

DEFINE LOGICAL DATA MODEL

The purpose of Define Logical Data Model process is to identify all uniquely distinguishable objects either used or produced by the system (the data entities), to capture all of the characteristics that help define those objects (the data attributes), and to describe the relationships between the entities. Like process modelling, definition of the data model can start as soon as the interviews or JAD sessions begin. A Data Process Modeler is most often responsible for designing the logical representation of the data to support the business need. Typically, this model will evolve throughout the iterations of capturing and documenting the business requirements.

The Data Modeler may begin to work on one of two paths: the first assumes that the application is brand new, and that the Data Modeler is working from a blank slate. In this case, informational requirements are captured as they are identified during the JAD sessions or interviews. As sessions are held, a view of potential entities and attributes is constructed and organized.

The key to successful data modelling is to ensure that the logical data model is not dependent on how the system processes the data. This ensures that data is grouped and organized based strictly on the informational needs of the system, and not based on an implied or assumed usage of the data by the system. The benefit is that the integrity of the data model will remain intact even if future business needs change the functionality of the system.

Defining the data model also helps to define the business rules by establishing the data entities (tables) and identifying attributes (fields). With the requirements and business rules known, and the Process Model outlined, the Project Team can begin to establish relationships between the data entities. This becomes the foundation of the data repository (or physical data model). As attributes are identified, the Data Modeler begins to build the Data Dictionary – again, in business English. Data normalization, a process in which complex relationships are simplified, is important once the Data Dictionary has been established. This eliminates redundancy, creates stable data structures, prevents anomalies, and simplifies data maintenance.

The Logical Data Model is the basis for the DBA to create the physical database, so it is important that the Data Dictionary is clear in its definitions and that all the data has been defined appropriately.

MAPPING BUSINESS REQUIREMENTS WITH MODELS

The purpose of Mapping Business Requirements with Models is to ensure that all business requirements and rules that have been captured have been accurately reflected and accommodated for in the Process Model and the Logical Data Model.

A typical technique at this point in the SDLC is to perform an analysis assessment, which validates and cross-references all requirements to the process and data models, and which continues until all gaps have been identified, resolved, or recognized as an out-of-scope item. One technique to reconcile the Business Requirements, Process Model and Logical Data Model is for the Business Analyst to create a gap analysis checklist or matrix that be used to display the interactions among the requirements, data entities and the processes. This will help to ensure that all the requirements have been captured and modelled appropriately.

It is helpful to walk Customers through this exercise so that they understand how all requirements have been captured and modelled. These reviews are often iterative, and any gaps identified are corrected through subsequent revisions to the Business Requirements, the Process Model, or the Logical Data Model. It may be necessary to hold several review sessions to go over the reconciliation with different sets of Customers, remembering that the more people who review the output, the less likely it will be that key elements have been missed. The Project Manager must ensure that the Customer understands the ramifications of overlooking a process, or of failing to decompose and model data appropriately. By understanding the potential impacts on both schedule and cost, the Customer is more likely to dedicate the appropriate staff to participate in these reviews.

FUNCTIONAL SPECIFICATION

Functional Specification is a document describing the logical grouping of related processes and functions within the new system, along with the mapping of these processes to both the business requirements that they satisfy and the data items with which they interact.

The ultimate goal of this process is to derive a comprehensive representation of the application that logically organizes related business processes, functions, data, and workflows. This provides a detailed roadmap from which the Customer Representatives can fully envision the final solution, and from which the Project Team can progress into the Design and Construction phases of the project lifecycle.

Whereas all System Requirements efforts up to this point have been focused on continually decomposing information into discrete requirements or processes that can each be reviewed and validated on their own merits, this final process now builds a broader view of the system that groups the individual pieces of the solution into logically related business functions. The final result, the Functional Specification, defines and illustrates how each requirement of the system will eventually be satisfied in terms of business processes (or transactions).

 # Functional Specification

Produce Functional Specification maps the Logical Data Model and Process Model to the organizations and locations of the business. This process produces the final deliverable for the phase – the Functional Specification.

Functional Specification
Document describing the logical grouping of related processes and functions within the new system, along with the mapping of these processes to both the business requirements that they satisfy and the data items with which they interact.

The Functional Specification will present many views of the system, from different perspectives and at different levels of detail. For example, the System Context Diagram shows how the new system fits into the larger picture of the Customer's application portfolio. The Business Flow Diagram shows how Customer and Consumer business units will interact with the new system from the business process and data flow perspectives.

And the System Interface Diagram will present a view of the system from a perspective of Consumer interface, depicting menu structures and navigation paths of online system components, and organization and distribution of reports and other batch interfaces.

Within the Functional Specification, each business process or transaction will correlate to the set of Business Requirements that it satisfies and a representation of the corresponding data elements. The reports associated with each process, business constraints (such as related security or controls), interfaces to other systems and business functions, and any related administrative operations required to support the system should also be identified.

Chapter 4 : SYSTEM DESIGN

The purpose of System Design is to create a technical solution that satisfies the functional requirements for the system. At this point in the project lifecycle there should be a Functional Specification, written primarily in business terminology, containing a complete description of the operational needs of the various organizational entities that will use the new system. The challenge is to translate all of this information into Technical Specifications that accurately describe the design of the system, and that can be used as input to System Construction.

The Functional Specification produced during System Requirements is transformed into a physical architecture. System components are distributed across the physical architecture, usable interfaces are designed and prototyped, and Technical Specifications are created for the Application Developers, enabling them to build and test the system.

THE PEOPLE

The skills needed by the Project Team to perform System Requirements analysis processes are dramatically different from those required to translate the requirements into a technical design. While it is certainly possible for the current team to possess the range of skills required for both phases, this assessment needs to be performed and the team profile adjusted to match the needs of System Design.

- Project Manager
- Project Sponsor
- Business Analyst
- Facilitator
- Data Process Modeler
- Technical Architect

- Quality Assurance
- Technical Support
- Information Security Officer
- Technical Support
- Customer Decision-Maker
- Customer Representative
- Stakeholders

DEFINE TECHNICAL ARCHITECTURE

The purpose of Define Technical Architecture is to describe the overall technical solution in terms of the hardware platform, programming development languages, and supporting toolsets to be used in the creation and maintenance of the new system. The goal of this effort is to design a technical solution and architecture to accommodate both the initial and expected long-term requirements of the Customer.

The Project Team needs to understand the processing and data management capabilities, and the respective long-term strategic technical directions, of the organization that will ultimately support this application. This understanding will enable the team to determine the best approach to distributing or centralizing the data and processing capabilities of the system.

 # Assess existing Infrastructure

The Project Team must perform a thorough assessment of the organization's existing infrastructure, standards, and information capabilities.

To define the technical architecture of the new system, the Project Team must perform a thorough assessment of the organization's existing infrastructure, standards, and information capabilities. Assuming that the technical platforms already in place can adequately support the new system, a design that leverages these existing platforms results in clear advantages in terms of increased productivity, decreased costs, and reduced learning curves. It is not uncommon, however, for new systems to impose technical solutions that require the extension or expansion of an organization's current architecture standards. Prime examples of this are organizations seeking to establish an Internet and Intranet presence with 24x7 accessibility, potentially introducing the necessity for new system support, security, disaster recovery, and maintenance strategies.

DEFINE SYSTEM STANDARDS

System Standards is a document detailing the various standards to be applied and adhered to throughout the execution of the project. Standards applicable to each phase of the lifecycle will be identified, along with examples, where applicable.

The purpose of the Define System Standards process is to develop and identify programming techniques, naming conventions, and all other standards that will be used to introduce consistency and conformity throughout system development efforts.

In an attempt to maximize efficiencies in the design, coding, testing and management of the system, it is important to define system standards early in the design process. System standards typically fall into three basic categories:

- Technical Development
- Configuration Management
- Release Management

Technical Development standards describe naming conventions, programming techniques, screen formatting conventions, documentation formats, and reusable components. These may be established for all projects in a large data processing/IT shop, or may be developed uniquely for a particular project. In addition, they may be unique to a development team, or industry standard and universally accepted.

Configuration Management standards provide the basis for management of the development of individual software components of the system. These standards ensure that functions such as controlling and tracking changes to the software being developed, along with backup and recovery strategies, are inherent in the development process.

DATABASE DESIGN

The purpose of the Database Design process is to accommodate all of the data that needs to be managed by the system within the system database tables and files. This information must be stored in a manner that ensures its reliability, accuracy, and completeness, while minimizing redundancy and meeting system performance expectations.

The Database Design process expands on the Logical Data Model created during System Requirements phase to identify physical database schemas, file formats, and data views required by the system. While the majority of new systems developed take advantage of relational database technologies, it is important to consider the feasibility of this approach for handling the full extent of the system's data needs.

Often, data will be used in the exchange of information between the system being developed and other existing legacy systems. The system interfaces may require the creation and management of data that, for valid reasons, uses other non-relational storage mechanisms. It is important to review existing database administration, data distribution, and data management policies and guidelines prior to proceeding with the definition of the physical database. These policies often dictate approaches to auditing, archiving, and recovering data that may need to be taken into consideration.

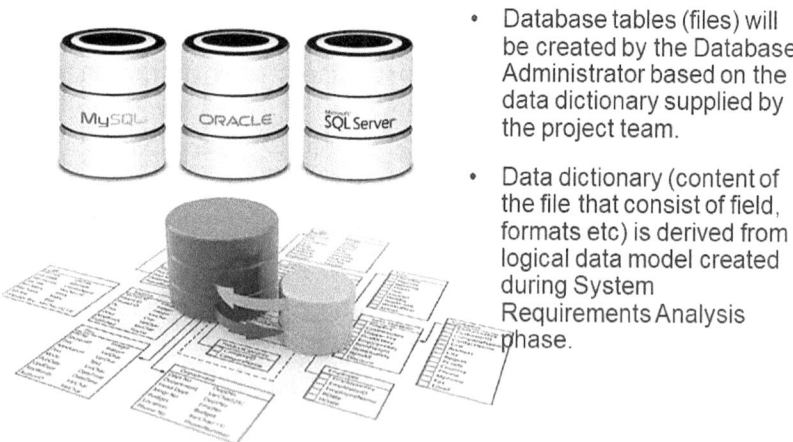

- Database tables (files) will be created by the Database Administrator based on the data dictionary supplied by the project team.

- Data dictionary (content of the file that consist of field, formats etc) is derived from logical data model created during System Requirements Analysis phase.

Database and System Files: Physical data storage repositories created to support the data management needs of the application being developed, either in the form of a relational database, tables, and structures, or in the form of structured system files.

PROTOTYPE SYSTEM COMPONENTS

The purpose of the Prototype System Components phase is two-fold – to provide early examples of system screens and reports that demonstrate to the Customer the proposed look and feel of the system; and to validate the applicability and feasibility of proposed technical components as they pertain to the overall technical solution.

Prototyping system components is one of the most popular methods used to help the Project Team to make educated design decisions based on an actual hands-on assessment of various alternatives. Prototyping also helps to mitigate the risks associated with the introduction of new technologies or toolsets into an organization. Often, throughout the design of a system, the Project Team may be faced with having to choose from several alternative approaches. They may have to select from a variety of technical architectures, package components, or graphical user interface (GUI) designs. In order to select the best approach for the project, it is necessary to determine what best meets the Customer's needs and expectations, and is technically feasible. Prototyping activities will often provide information on the performance and usability of the system, as well as insights into the design process.

Another benefit to prototyping is that by actively involving the Customers in the design of the system, a sense of ownership and buy-in is created that might not otherwise be possible, or that certainly could be more difficult to achieve if the system were designed without their input. In addition, there are advantages to engaging the Application Developers early in System Design.

While these developers will make their primary contribution to the project during System Construction, involvement during System Design will enhance their overall understanding of the system, the business objectives, and the rationale behind many of the design decisions, all of which will contribute towards a stronger final product.

WORK BREAKDOWN STRUCTURE

The project manager cannot complete this activity alone. A WBS is a graphical representation of the hierarchy of project deliverables and their associated tasks. As opposed to a Project Schedule that is calendar based, a WBS is deliverable-based, and written in business terms. All tasks depicted are those focused on completion of deliverables.

There are no dates or effort estimates in a WBS. Using a WBS, Project Team members are better equipped to estimate the level of effort required to complete tasks, and are able to quickly understand how their work fits into the overall project structure. The input and guidance of the project team is required as they are the individuals closest to the work and will be completing the actual activities within the project phases. The WBS will offer major input into planning, estimating, and scheduling processes throughout the project.

The first hierarchical level of a WBS usually contains the phases that are specific to the lifecycle of the project being performed. (For example, the first level of the WBS for a software development project would most likely contain System Requirements phase, System Design, etc.) For this reason, a WBS may be reused for other projects with the same lifecycle. Once the first level has been completed, it is broken down into more detailed sub-levels, until eventually all tasks are depicted. When defined to the appropriate level of detail, a WBS is very useful as input to both creating and refining a Project Schedule, including estimating required resources, level of effort, and cost.

A preliminary list of the roles and skills required to perform the necessary work (e.g., Architect, Team Leader) should be created at this stage in the project. This list will be refined in subsequent phases, as more becomes known about the project. Additional constraints, such as completion dates for project deliverables mandated by the Project Sponsor, Customer, or other external factors, will most often be known early in the project management lifecycle and should be noted. There may be financial, legal, or market-driven constraints that help dictate a project's high-level timeline.

Using the information from the WBS as input, the Project Manager should begin to document effort estimates, roles and dependencies, in preparation for creating a Project Schedule using a project management tool. It may also be helpful to solicit input from past Project Managers, Project Team members and subject matter experts for insight into past project performance, and to help uncover required activities, dependencies, and levels of effort.

DECOMPOSING THE PROJECT DELIVERABLES

Decomposition is the process of breaking down the major project deliverables into smaller, manageable components. So, what's a manageable component? It's a unit of the project deliverable that can be assigned resources, measured, executed, and controlled. So, how does one decompose the project deliverables? It's done this way:

The major deliverables of the project are identified. This includes the project management activities. A logical approach includes identifying the phases of the project life cycle or the major deliverables of the project.

Determine if adequate cost and time estimates can be applied to the lowest level of the decomposed work. Deliverables that won't be realized until later portions of the project may be difficult to decompose since there are many variables between now and when the deliverable is created. The smallest component of the WBS is the work package.

The lower-level items must be evaluated to ensure they are complete and accurate. Each item within the decomposition must be clearly defined and deliverable-orientated. Finally, each item should be decomposed to the point that it can be scheduled, budgeted, and assigned to a resource.

TESTING STRATEGY

Test plans created in the Produce Technical Specifications process define the overall strategy for validating the functionality of the system being developed, as well as the individual test cases that will be performed in the execution of this strategy. Additionally, the environments in which these tests will be executed must be defined in detail.

Four common types of testing are:

Unit Testing

where individual system components are independently tested as they are developed to ensure that each logic path contained within each module performs as expected. Many tests performed during unit testing can be used for more than one module (error handling, spell checking of screens and reports, etc.).

Integration Testing

where multiple, related elements of the system are tested together to validate components of the system, and to ensure that the appropriate edits and controls are functioning correctly. This testing concludes with the entire system being tested as a whole. "Bottom up" and/or "top down" testing approaches can be used. With bottom-up testing, the lowest level modules are created and tested first, and successive layers of functionality are added as they are developed. Top-down testing takes the opposite approach, where the highest-level modules are developed and tested, while lower level "stubs" are created and invoked until the actual modules are available. These stubs are temporary software modules that are created in order to enable the higher-level routines to be validated, but that do not yet perform the full set of functions needed by the system. Most testing strategies employ a mix of both approaches.

System Testing

where the entire system is linked together and tested to validate that it meets the operational requirements defined during System Requirements phase. Factors that are commonly tested at this level include performance, load, boundary, and external interfaces.

Acceptance Testing

where the Customer Representatives, and potentially Consumers and Stakeholders, perform validation tests to ensure that the developed system meets their expectations and needs. The results of this testing usually determine whether or not the system is ready to be released into production, so it is critical to define and understand the plan for completing this testing as early in the project as possible.

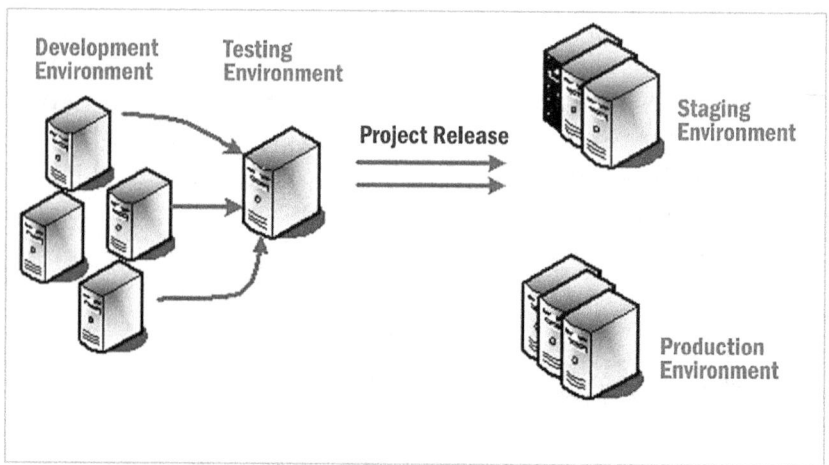

Thoroughly documented and detailed test cases provide two advantages. First, they enable the execution of these tests to be performed by any Project Team member, not just those team members that created the test cases. Secondly, they provide the basis for future regression testing efforts, where all aspects of system functionality are revalidated whenever changes are introduced to the system (most likely during the long-term maintenance and support of the system once it is in production). Involving the Quality Assurance Analyst in the development or review of these test cases can help to ensure that they can be leveraged by both the initial Project Team and the Customer once they have assumed ownership of the system.

DEFINE CHANGE CONTROL PROCESS

Every aspect of the project defined during System Initiation and System Design has the potential to change. In fact, change should be expected to occur throughout every project phase; but if an effective change control process is defined and agreed upon during System Design, any change should be able to be handled without negative effect on the project outcome. Project change is not defined simply as a change to the cost, end date, or Project

Scope. Change should be defined as ANY adjustment to ANY aspect of the Project Management plan or to any already approved deliverables. This includes anything formally documented in the Project Charter, Project Management plan, or any deliverable produced during the course of the project.

The Project Manager and Customer must agree on the change control process, which then must be formalized, documented, and included as a section in the Project Management plan.

Items that must be defined are:

- Identification of the individual(s) authorized to request a change.

- Identification of the person responsible for analyzing the request to understand its impact on the Project Cost, Scope, Schedule, and Quality, as well as the Customer Representative who has authority to approve the request. The Project Manager should never give the Project Team the go-ahead to begin work until a change request form has been signed by the Customer.

- The timeframe (number of business days) allowed for a change request to be approved or rejected by the Customer. It is important to document the fact that approval or rejection by default is not permitted, so acceptance or rejection cannot be assumed if there is no response to a submitted change request.

- The process to follow if no timely decision on approval or rejection of a change request is made. The Project Manager should follow up with the person to whom it was submitted to determine why the change request has not been processed.

- The percentage of the overall Project Budget that has been reserved for project changes. It is important to predetermine a change budget to prevent project work from being interrupted while funds are secured to do the work.

DEVELOP RISK MANAGEMENT PLAN

The Project Manager evaluates the results of the previous task to determine an appropriate response for each risk: avoidance, mitigation or acceptance. Each case will require a decision by the Project Team. The Project Manager is then responsible for communicating the steps necessary to manage the risk and following up with team members to ensure those steps are taken.

Since each risk may have more than one impact, the Risk Management Plan must describe the actions to be taken to avoid, mitigate or accept each risk impact, including **contingency plans**. It should also specify the individual responsible for the mitigation actions or contingency plan execution. Attention should be directed to those risks most likely to occur, with the greatest impact on the outcome of the project. On the other hand, a conscious decision can also be made by the Project Team to accept or ignore certain risks. These decisions must be documented as part of the Risk Management Plan for subsequent re-evaluations.

DEFINE ACCEPTANCE PROCESS

A detailed definition of each deliverable that will be produced during the course of the project is included in the Project Scope. A deliverable is considered complete when it has been accepted by the Customer. The Project Management plan must be revised to include a definition of the acceptance management process to be used for the project.

It is recommended that "acceptance" be defined as an authorized Customer decision maker's written approval signifying that a deliverable has meet expectations. It should be clearly stated that verbal acceptance or acceptance by default is not sufficient. To expedite the acceptance process, it is recommended that one individual per deliverable be given final decision-making authority. This person will be responsible for obtaining feedback from and representing the Customer.

In order for a deliverable to be considered "complete" and "acceptable," it must be measured against pre-determined acceptance criteria. The Project Manager and Customer must agree on the required criteria and the criteria must be documented and included in the Project Management plan. To ensure timely acceptance of deliverables, the Project Manager and Customer should agree on the format, content and appearance of deliverables before they are produced. This information should be documented and included in the Project Management plan. This helps to prepare the Customer to receive deliverables, and to avoid situations where deliverables are rejected because they do not meet Customer expectations. It is also important for the Project Manager to solicit feedback on deliverables throughout their development. Interim reviews of deliverables will streamline final acceptance.

In addition to acceptance criteria, the Project Manager and Customer must agree on, formalize, and document the deliverable acceptance process.

ISSUE MANAGEMENT PROCESS

Issue management involves capturing, reporting, escalating, tracking, and resolving problems that occur as a project progresses further. A process must be in place to manage issues, since they can potentially result in the need for change control and can become major problems if not addressed. The following items must be agreed upon between the Project Manager and Project Sponsor and must be documented and included as a section of the Project Management plan:

- How issues will be captured and tracked. Many Project Managers make use of some type of repository to ensure that issues are not lost. This repository that we called as Project Issues Register may be either electronic or manual, depending upon the needs and size of the project. At a minimum, Project Issues Register must contain a description of the issue, its potential impact, the date it is recorded, its anticipated closure date, its priority, and the name of the person responsible for resolving it or getting it resolved. The due date for closure must be a specific date (i.e., the date cannot be "ASAP"). As progress occurs on the resolution of an issue, the Project Manager should update the Project Issues Register to reflect what has occurred. Project Issues Register should be updated regularly, possibly as often as daily depending upon the needs of the project and issue resolution progress.

- How issues will be prioritized – the characteristics about the issue that will determine whether its resolution will be a high, medium or low priority. Impact to the schedule, level of effort, or cost are usually the factors that determine the priority.

- How and when issues will be escalated for resolution – whether they will be escalated if they are not resolved in a given period of time or when a delivery date is missed or only when the Project Budget is severely affected. Whatever the decision, details of the escalation process need to be clearly stated. It is also vital to document to whom issues will be escalated.

ORGANIZATIONAL CHANGE MANAGEMENT PLAN

When planning the project, the Project Manager and Customer must consider the impact the resulting product will have on the Customer. The organization must be prepared to accept and use the product once it is implemented. The Project Manager needs to define and document a plan to manage the changes to the organization that could occur as a result of implementing the product. This Organizational Change Management Plan becomes part of the Project Management plan. Organizational change management must be explicitly planned if it is to be effective.

People

The plan must consider how the individuals using the product will be affected by its implementation. The organization may initiate reductions or expansions in the workforce, and shift rote clerical activities to automated processing; decision-making power may be distributed further down the chain of command, or even regionally. If specific job duties are being added or removed, staff reductions or increases are anticipated, or the organizational structure itself will change, the plan must identify the steps to be taken. For example, the human resources manager in the Customer must be involved in planning for and performing many of these change management tasks.

Process

The plan must consider how the product of the project will affect already existing business processes in the Customer. Business processes may take advantage of streamlined workflows to reduce the flow of paper, or technology advances may enable electronic communications to more quickly deliver information. Procedures will need to be redesigned to align with the change. The new procedures may effect changes in the way the Customer develops, documents, and trains staff, and must be addressed in the Organizational Change Management Plan.

Culture

The plan must consider how severe the project's "culture shock" will be. The Project Manager must determine how much the project will affect the Customer's business strategy, established norms for performance, leadership approach, management style, approach to Customers, use of power, approach to decision making, and the role of the employee. Plans might include performing an assessment of the Customer's "readiness for change," and include development of action plans to increase the organization's readiness and ability to adapt to change through education and training. In cases where implementing a project will result in a significant change to the way an organization will conduct business, the Project Manager, Customer, and Project Sponsor must be able to anticipate when and how the major impacts will occur, and plan for the specific activities that will adequately prepare the Customer.

PROJECT BASELINE

A project baseline is a project "snapshot in time," taken at the conclusion of System Design, against which performance on the project is measured. Cost, Schedule, and Scope that have been verified will be used as the baselines where performance will be measured. It is one way the Project Manager can determine if the project is on track. Using project management tool, the project baselines are captured. Once the baseline version is approved, the Project Manager should revise it only if a change control is approved that results in a change to the schedule. The time, cost, and scope baselines become part of the Project Management plan. As the project progresses, subsequent schedules may be compared to the baseline version to track project performance.

DEVELOP PROJECT TEAM

To effectively perform the activities required to produce project deliverables, Project Team members must have appropriate levels of skill and knowledge. It is the job of the Project Manager to evaluate the skills of team members and determine whether or not they meet the current and future needs of the project. It is important to remember that there are many kinds of skills. Some are technical and others are "soft skills," such as management, presentation, and negotiation skills. If it is determined that the team needs training, the Project Manager must include training in the Project Schedule and Project Budget. Some skills can be learned on the job, some can be learned through informal mentoring, some can be learned using computer-based courses, and others may require formal classroom training.

When the training needs and the method of training for each team member have been determined and documented, the Project Manager or Team Leader documents the Training Plan, including a training schedule.

PROJECT TRANSITION PLAN

The Project Manager must formulate and document a plan for implementing or deploying the product of the project and for transitioning the responsibility for the outcome of the project from the Project Team to the Customer. The Transition Plan must include all the necessary activities to perform and procedures to follow to ensure a smooth and satisfactory hand-off. When planning the implementation and transition, the Project Team must consider the impact the resulting product will have on the Customer and Consumers. The Consumers must be prepared to use the product and the Customer must be prepared to support it.

The Project Manager needs to define and document a plan to implement the product, and should consider:

- What needs to be done to ensure the organization will be ready to receive the product. These steps may include acquiring the necessary physical space, installing appropriate software, obtaining the appropriate building permits, etc.
- How and when the Customer will test and accept the product and confirm and authorize its implementation.
- Procedures to ensure Consumers will be ready to use the product once it is transitioned. These steps must be coordinated with the Organizational Change Management Plan, and will include training and orientation on the use of the product.
- Developing plans for training Customers or Consumers as trainers for the future. The plan must define which of the

Customer require training, the level of training necessary, who will provide the training, and when it will occur.

- The appropriate strategy for implementing the product into the Customer, given the specific Consumers and Customers. For example, phased by location, phased by specific product functionality.
- Developing a plan to transition the ongoing support of the product to the Customer, to ensure that the appropriate individuals are ready to support the product once it has been implemented and is in use.

At the end of System Design, the Project Management plan should contain the following:

- Project Charter
- Project Scope
- Project Schedule
- Quality Plan
- Project Budget
- Risk Register
- Risk Management Plan
- Communications Management Plan
- Change Control Process
- Acceptance Management Plan
- Issue Management Process
- Organizational Change Management Plan
- Project Baseline
- Project Team Training Plan
- Project Implementation and Transition Plan

ACCEPTANCE PACKAGE

At this time, the Project Manager should schedule a meeting to discuss and gain agreement to secure resources for System Construction and System Acceptance. Meeting attendees should always include the Project Sponsor and the members of Customer Management whose resources will be affected. Attendees may also include members of other agencies who are able to provide resources that will add value during System Construction and System Acceptance. During the meeting, resources are formally secured by gaining the signatures of the appropriate Customer managers on the project deliverable approval form.

PROJECT SPONSOR APPROVAL

Before gaining an approval signature, the Project Manager must review the revised Business Case with the Project Sponsor. Based upon changes to the Business Case and policies within the Customer, the Project Sponsor must decide if a project re-approval cycle is warranted.

At this point in time, the Project Sponsor may decide to terminate the project. This decision may be based upon factors outside the control of the Project Manager (i.e., the organization may have new priorities that are in direct conflict with the project or increased risk may have been introduced to the project.) Or it is possible that, having done more detailed planning, the costs of doing the work are greater than initially estimated and outweigh any project benefits.

At the end of this task, the Project Manager must present the acceptance package to the Project Sponsor and obtain his/her signature, indicating approval to proceed to System Construction. If the Project Sponsor does not approve the package, he/she should indicate the reason for rejection. The Project Manager is then responsible for resolving issues with the deliverables and presenting the updated package to the Project Sponsor.

Chapter 5: SYSTEM CONSTRUCTION

PREPARE FOR SYSTEM CONSTRUCTION

The purpose of Prepare for System Construction is to get the technical environment and the Project Team members ready for successful completion of the full set of System Construction activities.

Prepare for System Construction

- Installation of System Development environment
- Installation of Testing environment
- Installation of Development Tools
- Installation of Software Version Control system
- Installation of User Acceptance Testing Environment
- Utilities to perform data extraction, transformation and loading (ETL) for data migration activities.

Much of the preparation for System Construction is completely analogous to that required for System Design, since these phases have many of the same characteristics, potentially expanding team size, introduction of new tools, and the establishment and communication of new processes that must be followed. As with prior phases, it may be necessary to revisit project orientation materials to confirm that pertinent information resulting from the completion of System Design is adequately communicated to individuals joining the team. Additionally, since new development tools and processes may be used in this phase, the training needs of both existing and new team members will need to be assessed.\

The Application Development Environment

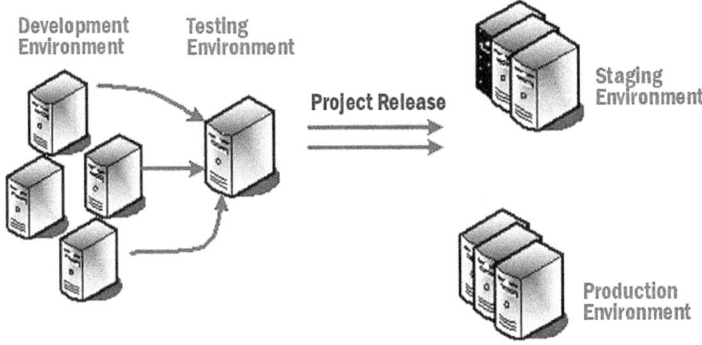

The Project Manager must make sure that the Project Team understands the purpose of new development, management, and testing tools, and the processes that need to be instituted for their use. As the team size grows, so does the potential for mistakes or miscommunications. System Construction often occurs at a point in the Project Schedule when the pressure of meeting deadlines increases. Shortcuts, whether intentional or not, may appear to provide attractive alternatives to meeting commitments. The need to adhere closely to defined procedures is, therefore, even more important than ever before. It should begin in the early stages of System Construction with the education of the team in the processes to be followed.

The start of System Construction marks a point in the project where the overall technical environment becomes more complex and more critical than in prior phases. Due to the scope of activities required to construct and test an application, having access to applicable tools such as automated software development tools, software configuration management tools, testing tools, and defect tracking tools can be extremely valuable to support these efforts.

Due to an increased dependence upon development tools, and the breadth and variety of technical environments that need to be established and supported, sufficient time must be taken at the start of this phase to make sure that these technical environments are correctly installed and configured. This marks the first phase in which it is necessary to institute multiple, distinct technical environments to accommodate the various construction and testing efforts.

The environments usually include:

- Development, where the individual team members perform their module construction and unit testing activities.

- Quality Assurance, where more universally controlled and managed integration and system testing efforts are conducted.

In System Acceptance, an "Acceptance Environment" is established that mimics the eventual Production state of the system, and which is able to support load and performance testing. Ultimately, a final Production environment will also be needed in which the system will operate once it has been deployed, but this is more traditionally established in System Implementation.

THE PEOPLE

The following roles are involved in carrying out the processes of this phase. Detailed descriptions of these roles can be found in the Glossary.

- Project Manager
- Project Sponsor
- Business Analyst
- Data Process Modeler
- Technical Architect

- Application Developers
- Technical Writer
- Software Quality Assurance
- Technical Support
- Information Security
- Technical Support (Help Desk, Documentation, Trainers)
- Customer Decision-Maker
- Customer Representative

BUILD, TEST, AND VALIDATE

The physical construction of the system components and utilities takes place during the Build portion of this process. In order to manage this effort, the Project Manager must have an exhaustive list of the modules to be built. With Tech Specs defining this list, development work can be logically partitioned (both in terms of identifying related work packets when distributing the work across the Project Team, and in terms of determining the sequence in which the development efforts will be approached), and progress can be measured and reported.

In order for the Application Developers to be able to code each module, they must have access to the Technical Specification associated with that module. Since it is likely that some of the Developers may not have been involved in creating these specs, the Business Analyst(s) should be available to answer questions dealing with the desired functionality and the Customer's intent behind the specs. Similarly, the Technical Lead should provide the technical background and expertise that the Application Developers may lack.

With unit test plans created during System Design, the individual who developed the code typically performs unit testing of each module. Establishing a process in which this unit testing is performed independent of the developer may improve the quality of the test, but may also be impractical given staffing or schedule limitations. It is important that this testing be performed thoroughly, to validate each of the logic paths the software module needs to support, and to capture the results of the tests for future reference. Unit testing is usually performed within the development environment; however, specific actions may need to be taken to ensure that this environment is initialized with the appropriate data and test tools. The test plans should identify any conditions required prior to the start of the unit testing efforts.

Validation consists of comparing the actual results of the testing against the expected results that were identified before any testing was performed. By putting these two sets of results side by side, the developer can determine if any corrections are required in the software. If so, another iteration of the build, test, and validate activities begins. This is also a point in the project when the Project Manager and Technical Lead must employ the concept of "peer reviews", in which team members review each other's code to confirm that the appropriate conventions and standards are being followed.

INTEGRATION AND SYSTEM TESTING

The purpose of Conduct Integration and System Testing is to continually validate larger and larger combinations of modules until the entire system is operating correctly as a single unit.

Having validated individual software components in Build, Test, and Validate, it is now time to begin validating the interaction among these components. The sequence and manner in which these software modules are combined should be defined in detail in the Integration Test Plans that were built during System Design. Where unit testing focused on the individual elements (as decomposed in the Technical Specifications), integration testing now needs to "roll up" the elements into logical groupings

(Integration Test Packets) and sub-systems (as identified in the Functional Specification).

Much of System Construction involves an iterative set of processes where the results of one activity may seed efforts in related activities. Results of integration testing may identify components of the system with defects that require re-execution of the Build/Test/Validate process; and once software modules have been modified and retested at the unit level, regression testing of the modules and any subsystems to which they pertain will again be required. This is often a good point in the project to begin to capture metrics relating to the quality of the system being developed. Data relating to the number of defects identified in testing, the types of defects, criticality, etc., can all be useful in understanding the state of the new system and attempting to evaluate deficiencies in the development processes being followed. For example, if the same errors are repeatedly detected from release to release, it may be an indication that aspects of the quality assurance processes being applied are not adequate, or that the unit tests for a particular module are not stringent enough to fully validate its functionality.

Ultimately, completion of this process should result in one of two conditions:

1. All Integration Tests have been successfully executed, demonstrating that the system performs to the expectations of the Project Team, or
2. The majority of Integration Tests have been successfully executed, identifying a known set of defects, which will require further resolution at some point in the future.

Should the latter situation arise, there may come a point at which it is appropriate for the Project Manager to discuss with the Customer the value of continuing this process at the expense of delaying the start of System Testing. If the known defects are relatively insignificant and do not prevent the system from satisfying the overall business objectives for which it was developed, it may be completely acceptable to initiate System Testing knowing that there may be some remaining Integration Testing issues to be resolved.

Chapter 6 :   SYSTEM ACCEPTANCE

System Acceptance is the point in the lifecycle at which every aspect of the application being developed, along with any supporting data conversion routines and system utilities, is thoroughly validated by the Customer Representatives prior to proceeding with System Implementation. This entire phase is centered on gaining sufficient evidence of the system's accuracy and functionality to be able to proceed to System Implementation with the highest level of confidence possible in the success of the system. This phase differs from System Construction in that acceptance testing is the final opportunity to establish that the system performs as expected in an environment that mimics production as closely as possible. In addition, while the Customer Representatives were certainly engaged throughout prior testing efforts, they now assume an even more critical role in the testing efforts in that they now need to exercise the system in the same way that they will once the full system is implemented. With the testing roadmap established in earlier lifecycle phases, the Customer Representatives now take responsibility for maneuvering the system through its operations.

Test / QA environment

A dedicated Test environment for testers and quality personnel to perform several testing activities that include:

- Applications functionality testing
- System Integration Testing
- Acceptance Testing
- Performance Testing
- Regression Testing

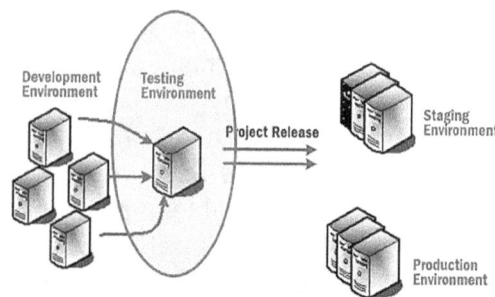

Test/QA environment must have similar working configuration with Production environment however performance capacity of the servers and database may be altered subject to the volume of transactions being tested.

In addition to confirming the operation of the system and it's fit to the business needs that it is intended to satisfy. System Acceptance is also the point in the lifecycle during which all supporting documentation and reference materials are updated to guarantee their consistency with the final delivered system.

PREPARE USER ACCEPTANCE TESTING ENVIRONMENT

The purpose of Prepare for User Acceptance Testing (UAT) Environment is to ensure that the testing environment to be used during System Acceptance is ready and operational, and to take any steps needed to prepare the acceptance testing team to successfully achieve their testing goals.

Preparation of both the testers and the environment in which they will operate is crucial to the success of this phase. User and training materials must be distributed in advance of this effort, and any training sessions needed to familiarize the testers with the application must be conducted.

In addition to familiarizing the testing team with the system, preparatory efforts must clarify for the team all testing roles and responsibilities, the timeline allocated to these efforts, and all processes to be followed regarding recording of testing results and reporting of defects. Although prior testing activities should have included Customer Representatives as part of the test team, it is common for this team to include an increased number of representatives so that real production operations can be better emulated. As a result, the testing team may now consist of participants who may not be as accustomed to rigorous testing activities as were members of the integration and system testing team, who typically have a more systems-oriented background. Therefore, expectations of these individuals need to be clearly defined, as do such elements as the testing strategy to be followed, the extent of testing to be performed, the definition of acceptance, etc.

TEST MANAGEMENT TEAM

One of the first steps in implementing a testing process is to consider the high-level organization of the staff involved in testing, their relationship to each other, and how the testing process will integrate with the existing management structure of the business. The guiding principle in establishing the high-level organization is that there are a series of activities common to all testing tasks which must be managed effectively and efficiently to ensure they are completed on time, on budget, and to an acceptable level of quality.

The challenge facing the majority of businesses involved in implementing a testing process is that testing cannot take place in isolation; there will be existing departments and groups within the company with which the testing process must integrate and existing staff who will need to participate in the testing process. For example, many businesses incorporate the management of the testing process into the existing information technology group. Alternatively, for businesses with a well-established quality culture, the testing process is often managed from within the quality assurance (QA) group.

Further issues that will need to be considered include the size and complexity of the business, the geographic distribution of offices, and the balance of software developed or extended in-house, developed under contract by a third party, and bought-in as commercial off-the-shelf (COTS) products. All of these factors will affect the size and role of the testing process within a particular business.

The capabilities of the testing team can greatly affect the success, or failure, of the testing effort. An effective testing team includes a mixture of technical and domain expertise relevant to the software problem at hand. It is not enough for a testing team to be technically proficient with the testing techniques and tools necessary to perform the actual tests. Depending on the complexity of the domain, a test team should also include members who have a detailed understanding of the problem domain. This knowledge enables them to create effective test artefacts and data and to effectively implement test scripts and other test mechanisms.

In addition, the testing team must be properly structured, with defined roles and responsibilities that allow the testers to perform their functions with minimal overlap and without uncertainty regarding which team member should perform which duties. One way to divide testing resources is by specialization in particular application areas and non-functional areas. The testing team may also have more role requirements than it has members, which must be considered by the test manager.

TEST MANAGER

The Test Manager has the authority to administer the organizational aspects of the testing process on a day-to-day basis and is responsible for ensuring that the individual testing projects produce the required products to the required standard of quality and within the specified constraints of time, resources, and costs. Where appropriate the Testing Manager is also responsible for liaison with the development teams to ensure that they follow the Unit and Integration Testing approach documented within the process. The Testing Manager will also liaise with the Independent Test Observer(s) to receive reports on testing projects that have failed to follow the testing process correctly.

The Testing Manager reports to a senior manager or director within the organization, such as the Quality Assurance (QA) Manager or Information Technology Director. In large organizations, and particularly those following a formal project management process, the Testing Manager may report to a Testing Program Board, which is responsible for the overall direction of the project management of the testing program.

TEST LEAD

The Test Team Leader is given the authority to run a testing project. His or her Responsibilities include tasking one or more Test Analysts and Testers, monitoring their progress against agreed-upon plans, setting up and maintaining the testing project filing system, and ensuring the generation of the testing project artifacts, including the Test Plan document, which will be used as the basis of project management control throughout the testing process.

TEST ENGINEER

- Designs and develops usability testing scenarios
- Administers usability testing process
- Proficient in designing test suites
- Understanding usability issues

- Defines criteria for performing usability testing, analyzes results of testing sessions, presents results to development team
- Skilled in test facilitation
- Develops test-product documentation and reports
- Excellent interpersonal skills
- Defines usability requirements, and interacts with customer to refine them
- Proficient in GUI design standards
- Participates in test-procedure walk-throughs
- Following is a typical list of expectations that must be communicated to testers.

Observe standards and procedures. The test engineer must be aware of standards and procedures to be followed, and processes must be communicated.

Keep schedules. Testers must be aware of the test schedule, including when test plans, test designs, test procedures, scripts, and other testing products must be delivered. In addition, the delivery schedule of software components to testing should be known by all testers.

Meet goals, and perform assigned tasks. Tasks must be documented and communicated, and deadlines must be scheduled, for each tester. The test manager and the test engineer must agree on the assigned tasks.

Meet budgets. For testers evaluating testing tools or other technology that must be purchased, the available budget must be communicated so the tester can work within that range and avoid wasting time evaluating products that are too expensive.

EVALUATION OF FUNCTIONAL TEST PROCEDURES

The following questions should be considered during an evaluation of functional test procedures:

- How completely are the test-procedure steps mapped to the requirements steps? Is traceability complete?
- Are the test input, steps, and output (expected result) correct?
- Are major testing steps omitted in the functional flow of the test procedure?
- Has an analytical thought process been applied to produce effective test scenarios?
- Have the test-procedure creation standards been followed?
- How many revisions have been required as a result of misunderstanding or miscommunication before the test procedures could be considered effective and complete?
- Have effective testing techniques been used to derive the appropriate set of test cases?

Software testing life cycle comprised of six processes:

1. Requirements Analysis
2. Test Planning
3. Test Case Development
4. Environment Setup
5. Test Execution
6. Test Cycle Closure

 ## Software Testing Life Cycle

Following steps are involved in Software Testing Life Cycle (STLC). Each step is to have its own Entry Criteria and deliverable.

- Requirement Analysis
- Test Planning
- Test Case Development
- Environment Setup
- Test Execution
- Test Cycle Closure

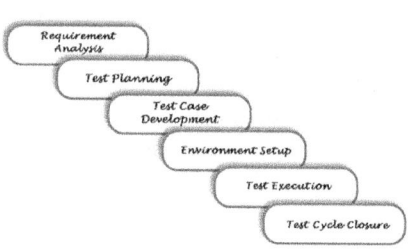

Planning must take place as early as possible in the software life cycle, because lead times must be considered for implementing the test program successfully. Gaining an understanding of the task at hand early on is essential in order to estimate required resources, as well as to get the necessary buy-in and approval to hire personnel and acquire testing tools, support software, and hardware. Early planning allows for testing schedules and budgets to be estimated, approved, and then incorporated into the overall software development plan. Lead times for procurement and preparation of the testing environment, and for installation of the system under test, testing tools, databases, and other components must be considered early on. No two testing efforts are the same. Effective test planning requires a clear understanding of all parts that can affect the testing goal. Additionally, experience and an understanding of the testing discipline are necessary, including best practices, testing processes, techniques, and tools, in order to select the test strategies that can be most effectively applied.

During test-strategy design, risks, resources, time, and budget constraints must be considered. An understanding of estimation techniques and their implementation is needed in order to estimate the required resources and functions, including number of personnel, types of expertise, roles and responsibilities, schedules, and budgets.

Understanding the task at hand, its scope, and its associated testing goals are the first steps in test planning. Test planning requires a clear understanding of every piece that will play a part in achieving the testing goal.

Test plans created in the System Construction phase define the overall strategy for validating the functionality of the system being developed, as well as the individual test cases that will be performed in the execution of this strategy. Additionally, the environments in which these tests will be executed must be defined in detail.

TESTING STRATEGY

Test plans created in the Produce Technical Specifications process define the overall strategy for validating the functionality of the system being developed, as well as the individual test cases that will be performed in the execution of this strategy. Additionally, the environments in which these tests will be executed must be defined in detail.

UNIT TESTING

Unit Testing, where individual system components are independently tested as they are developed to ensure that each logic path contained within each module performs as expected. Many tests performed during unit testing can be used for more than one module (error handling, spell checking of screens and reports, etc.).

 ## Unit Testing

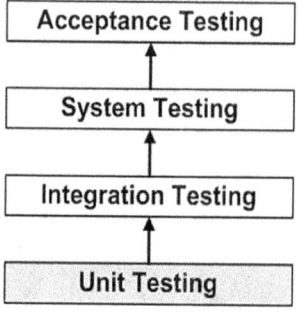

- **Unit Testing** is a level of software testing where individual units/components of a software are tested.
- The purpose is to validate that each unit of the software performs as designed.
- A unit is the smallest testable part of software. It usually has one or a few inputs and usually a single output. In procedural programming a unit may be an individual program, function, procedure, etc.

Unit Testing is the first level of testing and is performed prior to Integration Testing. Unit Testing is normally performed by software developers themselves or their peers. In rare cases it may also be performed by independent software testers.

INTEGRATION TESTING

Integration Testing, where multiple, related elements of the system are tested together to validate components of the system, and to ensure that the appropriate edits and controls are functioning correctly. This testing concludes with the entire system being tested as a whole. "Bottom up" and/or "top down" testing approaches can be used. With bottom-up testing, the lowest level modules are created and tested first, and successive layers of functionality are added as they are developed. Top-down testing takes the opposite approach, where the highest-level modules are developed and tested, while lower level "stubs" are created and invoked until the actual modules are available. These stubs are temporary software modules that are created in order to enable the higher-level routines to be validated, but that do not yet perform the full set of functions needed by the system. Most testing strategies employ a mix of both approaches.

 **Integration testing**

- **Integration Testing** is a level of software testing where individual units are combined and tested as a group.
- The purpose of this level of testing is to expose defects in the interfaces and in the interactions between integrated components or systems

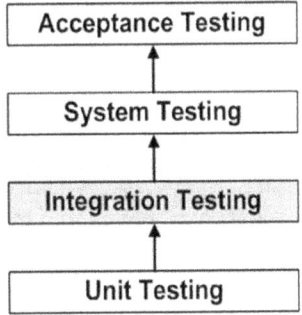

Integration Testing is performed after Unit Testing and before System Testing.

Developers themselves or independent Testers perform Integration Testing.

SYSTEM TESTING

System Testing, where the entire system is linked together and tested to validate that it meets the operational requirements defined during System Requirements phase. Factors that are commonly tested at this level include performance, load, boundary, and external interfaces.

System testing

- **System Testing** is a level of the software testing where a complete and integrated software is tested.
- The purpose of this test is to evaluate the system's compliance with the specified requirements.
- The process of testing an integrated system to verify that it meets specified requirements.

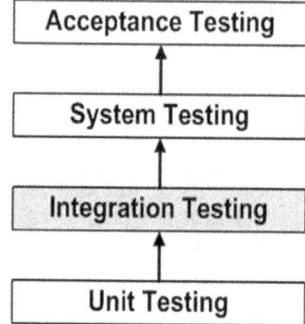

System Testing is performed after Integration Testing and before Acceptance Testing.

Normally, independent Testers perform System Testing.

ACCEPTANCE TESTING

Acceptance Testing, where the Customer Representatives, and potentially Consumers and Stakeholders, perform validation tests to ensure that the developed system meets their expectations and needs. The results of this testing usually determine whether or not the system is ready to be released into production, so it is critical to define and understand the plan for completing this testing as early in the project as possible.

 **Acceptance testing**

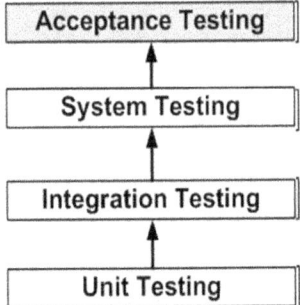

- **Acceptance Testing** is a level of the software testing where a system satisfies the acceptance criteria and to enable the user, customers or other authorized entity to determine whether or not to accept the system.
- The purpose of this test is to evaluate the system's compliance with the business requirements and assess whether it is acceptable for delivery.

Acceptance Testing is performed after System Testing and before making the system available for actual use.

Thoroughly documented and detailed test cases provide two advantages. First, they enable the execution of these tests to be performed by any Project Team member, not just those team members that created the test cases. Secondly, they provide the basis for future regression testing efforts, where all aspects of system functionality are revalidated whenever changes are introduced to the system (most likely during the long-term maintenance and support of the system once it is in production). Involving the Quality Assurance Analyst in the development or review of these test cases can help to ensure that they can be leveraged by both the initial Project Team and the Customer once they have assumed ownership of the system.

Prepare for System Construction

The purpose of Prepare for System Construction is to get the technical environment and the Project Team members ready for successful completion of the full set of System Construction activities.

Much of the preparation for System Construction is completely analogous to that required for System Design, since these phases have many of the same characteristics, potentially expanding team size, introduction of new tools, and the establishment and communication of new processes that must be followed. As with prior phases, it may be necessary to revisit project orientation materials to confirm that pertinent information resulting from the completion of System Design is adequately communicated to individuals joining the team. Additionally, since new development tools and processes may be used in this phase, the training needs of both existing and new team members will need to be assessed.

The Project Manager must make sure that the Project Team understands the purpose of new development, management, and testing tools, and the processes that need to be instituted for their use. As the team size grows, so does the potential for mistakes or miscommunications. System Construction often occurs at a point in the Project Schedule when the pressure of meeting deadlines increases. Shortcuts, whether intentional or not, may appear to provide attractive alternatives to meeting commitments. The need to adhere closely to defined procedures is, therefore, even more important than ever before. It should begin in the early stages of System Construction with the education of the team in the processes to be followed.

The start of System Construction marks a point in the project where the overall technical environment becomes more complex and more critical than in prior phases. Due to the scope of activities required to construct and test an application, having access to applicable tools such as automated software development tools, software configuration management tools, testing tools, and defect tracking tools can be extremely valuable to support these efforts.

Due to an increased dependence upon development tools, and the breadth and variety of technical environments that need to be established and supported, sufficient time must be taken at the start of this phase to make sure that these technical environments are correctly installed and configured. This marks the first phase in which it is necessary to institute multiple, distinct technical environments to accommodate the various construction and testing efforts.

The environments usually include:

- Development, where the individual team members perform their module construction and unit testing activities.
- Quality Assurance, where more universally controlled and managed integration and system testing efforts are conducted.

In System Acceptance, an acceptance environment is established which mimics the eventual Production state of the system, and which is able to support load and performance testing. Ultimately, a final Production environment will also be needed in which the system will operate once it has been deployed, but this is more traditionally established in System Implementation.

The People

The following roles are involved in carrying out the processes of this phase. Detailed descriptions of these roles can be found in the Glossary.

- Project Manager
- Project Sponsor
- Business Analyst
- Data Process Modeler
- Technical Architect
- Application Developers
- Technical Writer
- Software Quality Assurance
- Technical Support
- Information Security
- Technical Support (Help Desk, Documentation, Trainers)

- Customer Decision-Maker
- Customer Representative

Build, Test, and Validate

The physical construction of the system components and utilities takes place during the Build portion of this process. In order to manage this effort, the Project Manager must have an exhaustive list of the modules to be built. With Tech Specs defining this list, development work can be logically partitioned (both in terms of identifying related work packets when distributing the work across the Project Team, and in terms of determining the sequence in which the development efforts will be approached), and progress can be measured and reported.

In order for the Application Developers to be able to code each module, they must have access to the Technical Specification associated with that module. Since it is likely that some of the Developers may not have been involved in creating these specs, the Business Analyst(s) should be available to answer questions dealing with the desired functionality and the Customer's intent behind the specs. Similarly, the Technical Lead should provide the technical background and expertise that the Application Developers may lack.

With unit test plans created during System Design, the individual who developed the code typically performs unit testing of each module. Establishing a process in which this unit testing is performed independent of the developer may improve the quality of the test, but may also be impractical given staffing or schedule limitations. It is important that this testing be performed thoroughly, to validate each of the logic paths the software module needs to support, and to capture the results of the tests for future reference. Unit testing is usually performed within the development environment; however, specific actions may need to be taken to ensure that this environment is initialized with the appropriate data and test tools. The test plans should identify any conditions required prior to the start of the unit testing efforts.

Validation consists of comparing the actual results of the testing against the expected results that were identified before any testing was performed. By putting these two sets of results side by side, the developer can determine if any corrections are required in the software. If so, another iteration of the build, test, and validate activities begins. This is also a point in the project when the Project Manager and Technical Lead must employ the concept of "peer reviews", in which team members review each other's code to confirm that the appropriate conventions and standards are being followed.

Integration and System Testing

The purpose of Conduct Integration and System Testing is to continually validate larger and larger combinations of modules until the entire system is operating correctly as a single unit.

Having validated individual software components in Build, Test, and Validate, it is now time to begin validating the interaction among these components. The sequence and manner in which these software modules are combined should be defined in detail in the Integration Test Plans that were built during System Design. Where unit testing focused on the individual elements (as decomposed in the Technical Specifications), integration testing now needs to "roll up" the elements into logical groupings (Integration Test Packets) and sub-systems (as identified in the Functional Specification).

Much of System Construction involves an iterative set of processes where the results of one activity may seed efforts in related activities. Results of integration testing may identify components of the system with defects that require re-execution of the Build/Test/Validate process; and once software modules have been modified and retested at the unit level, regression testing of the modules and any subsystems to which they pertain will again be required. This is often a good point in the project to begin to capture metrics relating to the quality of the system being developed. Data relating to the number of defects identified in testing, the types of defects, criticality, etc., can all be useful in understanding the state of the new system and attempting to evaluate deficiencies in the development processes being followed. For example, if the same errors are repeatedly detected from release to release, it may be an indication that aspects of the quality assurance processes being applied are not adequate, or that the unit tests for a particular module are not stringent enough to fully validate its functionality.

Ultimately, completion of this process should result in one of two conditions:

1. All Integration Tests have been successfully executed, demonstrating that the system performs to the expectations of the Project Team, or
2. The majority of Integration Tests have been successfully executed, identifying a known set of defects, which will require further resolution at some point in the future

Should the latter situation arise, there may come a point at which it is appropriate for the Project Manager to discuss with the Customer the value of continuing this process at the expense of delaying the start of System Testing. If the known defects are relatively insignificant and do not prevent the system from satisfying the overall business objectives for which it was developed, it may be completely acceptable to initiate System Testing knowing that there may be some remaining Integration Testing issues to be resolved.

MANAGE ACCEPTANCE

The goal of this task is to manage the acceptance of project deliverables according to the acceptance management process developed during System Design. The acceptance management process is part of the Project Management plan, and documents:

- The definition of "acceptance"
- The criteria that must be met for each deliverable to be considered "acceptable"
- The number and identity of Customers designated to be reviewers of each deliverable
- The number and identity of Customers designated to be approvers – approvers have the authority to sign the approval form, indicating acceptance
- The number of business days in which deliverables must be either approved or rejected by the reviewers and approvers
- The number of times a deliverable can be resubmitted
- The escalation process that will be followed if a timely decision on approval or rejection of a deliverable is not met

Acceptance begins when the Project Manager presents a completed deliverable and Project Deliverable Approval Form to the approver. When logistically possible, the Project Manager must take the time to formally review the deliverable, in person, with the approver. In some cases, the approver's geographic location or work shift prohibits face-to-face communication. Where in-person communication is feasible, it is recommended that the Project Manager not simply send the deliverable via email or leave it on the approver's desk. If the Project Manager has done a very thorough job in setting expectations, the approver may indicate acceptance at the end of this face-to-face presentation.

More likely, however, the approver will prefer to have designated reviewers examine the document or product and recommend a course of action.

The reviewers independently analyze the deliverable and produce a recommendation as to whether to accept the deliverable, providing their comments and signature on the accompanying approval form. This must be done within the turnaround time documented in the acceptance management process. If a reviewer recommends the deliverable be rejected, he/she must provide the reason and forward the package back to the approver. This process should be followed for each person designated as a reviewer in the Acceptance Management Plan.

Chapter 7 : SYSTEM IMPLEMENTATION

During System Design, the Project Manager formulated and documented a plan for implementing or deploying the product of the project, and for transitioning the responsibility for the outcome of the project from the Project Team to the Customer. During System Construction, this Implementation and Transition Plan will be more fully developed as the product of the project is developed, and as specific activities in the plan are executed. During System Construction, the Project Team will gain a better understanding of the impact the resulting product will have on the Customer and Consumers. Activities begin that are required to prepare the Consumers to use the product, along with the tasks to prepare the Customer to support it. Managing Implementation and Transition includes:

- Monitoring and ensuring timely completion of all facilities issues, such as acquiring the necessary physical space, installing appropriate software, obtaining the appropriate building permits, etc.

- Coordinating Customer Acceptance Testing, including logistics of when and how Customers will test the product to confirm that it meets requirements before it is formally implemented and transitioned. Customer testing is one of the last opportunities for necessary changes to be identified and made to the product before rollout. Time for sufficient Customer testing and any resulting rework that will affect the Project Team must be incorporated in the Project Schedule.

- Managing the steps that need to be taken to ensure Consumers will be ready to use the product once it is implemented. These steps must be coordinated with the Organizational Change Management Plan, and will include training and orientation on the use of the product. Any training for Customers or Consumers must be provided according to the plan and coordinated with other aspects of the implementation of the product.

- Managing the detailed implementation. The Project Manager must monitor implementation activities and make any necessary adjustments. The implementation will vary depending upon the needs of the Customer and the product of the project. Some implementations are "done" at the flip of the final switch, such as opening a new highway, or publishing a book. Others are phased into implementation, like installing an inventory management system module-by-module, moving to a new building floor-by-floor, or implementing a new business process location-by-location.

Managing the steps that need to be taken to ensure the appropriate individuals are ready to support the product once it has been implemented and is in use. This may include negotiating with various internal organizations to determine the appropriate timing of the transition of responsibility, assigning specific organizations and individuals to support the specific products, and providing necessary training. The Project Manager must carefully manage the point in implementation that the Customer takes responsibility for production problems, "help" or trouble calls, and for resolving the problems, and ensure that all pre-requisites for transition have been met for example, performance standards, quality standards, etc.

TRANSITION MANAGEMENT

The purpose of Transition Management is to formally acknowledge that all deliverables produced during System Acceptance have been completed, tested, accepted, and approved by the project's Customers and the Project Sponsor, and that the product or service the project developed was successfully transitioned from the Project Team to the Customer.

Formal acceptance and approval also signify that the project is essentially over, and is ready for System Implementation. Once the product of the project has been successfully transitioned to the Customer, the Project Manager should prepare the final status report and conduct the final status meeting. The Project Schedule must be up to date for all completed project and project management lifecycle phases.

This is the final opportunity for all participants to confirm that the product of the project has been successfully developed and transitioned. Any outstanding issues or action items must be transitioned from the Project Team to the Customer.

As the deliverables of the project are produced and accepted, approval signatures are gained from the Project Sponsor and Customer Decision-Makers. Following the final status meeting, the Project Manager must obtain the Project Sponsor's signature one final time, indicating acceptance of the project to date, and indicating approval to proceed to System Implementation.

CLOSING THE PROJECT

The purpose of closing the project (project closure) is to assess the project and derive any lessons learned and best practices to be applied to future projects. Project closure begins with a Post-Implementation Review. The review may start with a survey designed to solicit feedback on the project from the Project Team, Customers, Consumers and other stakeholders. Once feedback has been collected and evaluated, an assessment meeting is conducted to derive best practices and formulate lessons learned to inform future efforts. Ideally, the best practices and lessons learned should be stored in a centralized organizational repository, facilitating access and retrieval by managers of future projects.

Project closure ends with administrative closeout providing feedback on Project Team members, updating the skills inventory, capturing key project metrics, and filing all pertinent project materials into the project repository.

Conduct Post-Implementation Review

A project is considered complete when it has been successfully implemented and transitioned to the Customer and approved by the Project Sponsor. At this point in the project management lifecycle, the responsibilities of the Project Manager are to assess how closely the project met Customer needs, highlight what worked well, learn from mistakes made during the project, identify patterns and trends, derive ways to improve upon processes executed throughout the project, and, most importantly, communicate results. The purpose of Conduct Post-Implementation Review is to gather the information required to meet those responsibilities, and to present the information in a Post-Implementation Report.

The most important measures of the success of a project are whether the product was developed and delivered successfully and how well the needs of the Customers have been met. The most effective way to determine these measures is to Solicit Feedback. The Project Manager should gather feedback using a survey appropriate to the project. Depending on the size and type of the project and the structure of the Customer, different surveys may be required for different stakeholder groups, and surveys will need to be distributed to the appropriate individuals. At a minimum, feedback should be solicited from the Project Sponsor and Project Team members who performed the tasks in the Project Schedule. The Project Manager should determine if surveys should also be given to Customer Representatives, or other stakeholders in order to collect sufficient information for assessing the success of the project in meeting its goals and their needs. The survey must also assess the outcome of the project and the performance of the Project Team and Customer. The Project Manager must stress to all survey participants the importance of their honest feedback as one of the primary mechanisms for assessing the project's performance.

CONDUCT PROJECT ASSESSMENT

The goal of this task is for the Project Manager to meet with select members of the Project Team and stakeholder community to present the summarized results of the feedback surveys, discuss all other aspects of the completed project, gain consensus on what was successful and what was not, and derive best practices and lessons learned. In addition to the Project Team, the Project Manager should consider inviting Project Managers from the Customer with experience on similar projects. Based on experience and prior knowledge, other Project Managers can provide information and insight on the assessment process. It is a good idea for the Project Manager to distribute the summarized survey results to each participant in advance of the Project Assessment Meeting, to allow them to come prepared to address the contents.

In order to provide the best possible products and services to Customers, Customer Management must strive to continuously improve the way projects are managed and products are delivered. During the course of the assessment meeting, participants will consider the summarized feedback results and the experience of the Project Managers in attendance to discuss and assess the performance of the project. Based upon these discussions, the group will identify and agree upon lessons learned. These lessons will not only benefit the current Project Team, they will also help managers and team members of similar projects. The lessons may be positive or negative. Lessons learned must not simply be identified during the meeting. It is also important to document each one and develop an action plan describing when and how they might be implemented within the Customer.

PERFORM ADMINISTRATIVE CLOSEOUT

The purpose of Perform Administrative Closeout is to perform all administrative tasks required to bring the project to an official close.

Throughout the course of the project, the Project Manager maintained a project repository. As the project progressed, the purpose of the repository was to create a central point of reference for all project materials to be used by anyone involved in the project. Once the project comes to an official close, the repository provides an audit trail documenting the history and evolution of the project.

During project closure, the Project Manager should examine the repository to ensure that all relevant project-related material, documents produced, decisions made, issues raised and correspondence exchanged have been captured. In addition, the Post-Implementation Report should be included. When the project is officially closed, the project repository should include the following materials:

- Project supporting documentation, including the Business Case and Project Proposal
- Project description/definition documents such as the Project Charter and Project Management plan
- Any working documents or informal documents defining Cost, Scope, Schedule and Quality of the project
- Project Schedules: retain all copies electronically, but only include the baseline and final schedule in the hardcopy repository
- Project financials
- Project Scope changes and requests log
- Project Status Reports
- Team member progress reports and timesheets
- Issue's log and details (open and resolved)
- Project acceptance log by deliverable

- Project Deliverable Approval Forms, with original signatures
- Risk Management Worksheets
- Audit results, if encountered
- Correspondence, including any pivotal or memos, letters, email, etc.
- Meeting notes
- Final Project Acceptance Form, with original signatures
- Post-Implementation Report

Chapter 8 :   PROJECT COMMUNICATION

Formalized regular reporting on the status of the project is an integral part of the quality management of the project. In order to make appropriate decisions, the Steering Committee, Project Sponsor or Senior Manager needs to be informed properly about the status of the project. The Project Manager should establish this reporting as part of the management activities for the project.

In this chapter, you will learn about developing an effective communications plan to better track, monitor, and report the project's progress. After studying this chapter, you should understand and be able to:

- Identify and describe the processes associated with the project management body of knowledge area called project communications management, which includes project communications planning, information distribution, performance reporting, and administrative closure.

- Describe several types of reporting tools that support the communications plan.

- Apply the concept of earned value and discuss how earned value provides a means of tracking and monitoring a project's scope, schedule, and budget.

- Describe how information may be distributed to the project stakeholders and the role information technology plays to support the project communications.

Information technology projects historically have demonstrated a poor track record for a variety of reasons. Often unrealistic Project Management plans are created from inaccurate estimates, and, as a result, projects have little chance of achieving their objectives. As you saw earlier, various tools and techniques for estimating IT projects exist; but consistently developing accurate and realistic estimates remains a challenge. Much of an organization's capability to consistently and accurately estimate IT projects lies with well-defined processes, experience, and an information base of past projects. Still, developing a realistic and effective Project Management plan is only part of the solution.

The project manager must also have a clear picture of how the actual progress or work compares to the original baseline plan. Seldom do things go according to plan, so the project manager must have the means to monitor and manage the project. This will allow him or her to make well-informed decisions, take appropriate actions when necessary, or make adjustments to the Project Management plan.

Communication is important for successful project management. The PMBOK area called project communications management includes:

COMMUNICATIONS PLANNING

Communications planning attempts to answer the following questions:

- How will information be stored?
- How will knowledge be stored?
- What information goes to whom, when, and how?
- Who can access what information?
- Who will update the information and knowledge?
- What media of communication is best?

Information Distribution: Focuses on getting the right information to the right people in the right format. Moreover, information distribution should also include organizing minutes from meetings and other project related documents.

Performance Reporting: Focuses on the collection and dissemination of project information to the various project stakeholders. This should include status reports, progress reports, and forecast reports.

Administrative Closure: Focuses on verifying and documenting the project's progress. This includes organizing and archiving project records and lessons learned.

PROJECT COMMUNICATIONS PLAN

A project communications plan should include not only the information content for each stakeholder, but also the delivery of this information. Although a great deal of information can be obtained or distributed informally, the communications plan should detail the way data will be collected and the form in which information will be provided. Although an opportunity exists for capturing and disseminating data and information, an IT-based solution may not be practical or effective in all situations. For example, e-mail is a powerful tool for communication; however, richer forms of communication, such as face-to-face meetings, may be more appropriate or effective in certain situations.

Developing a communications plan starts with identifying the various stakeholders of the project and their information needs. Recall that stakeholder analysis helps the project manager and project team determine the different interests and roles of each of the stakeholders. Although some of the information contained in the stakeholder analysis may not be suitable for general dissemination, it provides a starting point for identifying who needs what information and when.

MANAGE COMMUNICATIONS

Project status reporting is regular, formalized reporting on the progress of the project against the Project Management Plan.

Usually, it is reported by the Project Manager to the Project Steering Committee, Project Sponsor or Senior Manager, depending on the size and management structure of the project. Status reporting also can be to individuals or committees that are contributing to the work of the project, such as Reference or Working Groups, Quality Consultants etc.

PURPOSE OF THE PROJECT STATUS REPORT

Formalized regular reporting on the status of the project is an integral part of the quality management of the project. In order to make appropriate decisions, the Steering Committee, Project Sponsor or Senior Manager needs to be informed properly about the status of the project. The Project Manager should establish this reporting as part of the management activities for the project.

Another purpose for the Project Status Report is to provide an ongoing history of the project, which becomes very useful in terms of tracking progress, evaluation and review. Project Status Reports form part of the project review processes, both during and after completion of the project.

The Project Status Report is a document that is used by the Project Manager for formalized regular reporting on the status of the project to the Steering Committee, Project Sponsor, Senior Manager or other Key Stakeholders.

Depending on the size of the project, the substance of the report is based on:

- Regular review of project progress, against the Project Management plan, at Project Team planning meetings
- Sub-project status reports to the Project Manager, in the case of large projects
- Regular review of project progress against the milestones in the approved Project Business Plan

- Regular meetings with the Project Sponsor/Senior Manager
- Regular review of the effectiveness of actions as outlined in the Risk Management Plan, and their effect on the grades for likelihood and seriousness for project risks
- Regular review of the Issues Register
- Regular review of progress against budget
- Regular updating of milestones

STRUCTURE OF PROJECT STATUS REPORT

While the Project Sponsor/Steering Committee should agree to the proposed structure of the Project Status Report and frequency of reporting to them, the report should include, as a minimum, the following:

Status of the project: description; milestones for the last reporting period; milestones for the next reporting period; impact of achievement/non-achievement of milestones for the remaining period of the project

- **Budget Report** - with respect to planned expenditure, actual expenditure deficit/surplus and revenue against planned output delivery, if appropriate
- **Risk Management Report** - specifying any changes to the major risks identified since the previous report, and modification to the strategies put in place to manage them; any new risks that have arisen since the last report, as identified in the Risk Register
- **Issues Report** - including areas of concern, specific problems and any action/decision that needs to be taken by the Steering Committee or Project Sponsor/Senior Manager, as identified in the Issues Register

- Any general information
- Recommendations

It is important to keep the report focused, and to report on/against milestones, not percentage of work completed. A milestone can be defined as a progress marker that identifies when significant points in a project have been reached. Milestones are anchored within the timeframe for the project, and reflect the critical path towards the final delivery of the outputs. If milestone slippage is occurring it could be a danger sign that the project will not be completed within the specified timeframe.

ISSUES MANAGEMENT

Management of project issues focuses on monitoring, reviewing and addressing issues or concerns as they arise through the life of a project. Issues can be raised by anyone involved with the project, including the Business Owners, Steering Committee members, Reference or Working Group members, the Project Manager, Project Team members and other Key Stakeholders.

For small projects, a brief scan and ongoing monitoring may be all that is required. In large and/or more complex projects, it is advisable to maintain a Project Issues Register. From this register the issue, current status and resolution, where appropriate, should be reported regularly to the Steering Committee as part of the Project Status Report.

A Project Issues Register should be established as part of the ongoing project management activities. The Project Manager and Team need to have a process for capturing issues as they arise, updating and reviewing them so that they can be managed and resolved as the project moves forward. Once a resolution is agreed on, the appropriate activities are added to the project work plan to ensure the issue is resolved, and to the project budget if appropriate.

If the project is medium to large or quite complex, separate Project Issues Registers might be established for each of the major outputs as they are being developed. If an issue cannot be resolved it could become a risk, and if identified as such should be added to the Risk Register. Small projects also can benefit from the establishment of a Project Issues Register, as it is low maintenance and high value in terms of keeping the project on track and managing the issues, preferably before they become risks.

A Project Issues Register is basically a form, often in a MS Word® table, for the systematic recording of issues. It usually contains the following for each issue:

- A unique number
- A description
- Who raised the issue?
- Date reported
- Priority rating
- The person or group responsible for resolving the issue
- How it is resolved (included as an action in the project work plan and budget, documented in the Project Issues Register or closed)
- Status, usually open or closed
- Date resolved

Project Team meetings should include, on the agenda, a review of current issues for each meeting. Current issues should be reported in the Project Status Report. In the case of a small project, it may be a verbal discussion between the Project Manager and Project Sponsor/Senior Manager.

If it is unclear as to whether an item belongs on the Project Issues Register, or is something that needs to be dealt with, but will not impede the project, it can be recorded on an action list kept by the Project Team until resolved.

Chapter 9 : PROJECT GOVERNANCE

Project Sponsor

The project sponsor is a manager with a demonstrable interest in the outcome of the project who is responsible for securing spending authority and resources for the project. Ideally, the project sponsor should be the highest-ranking manager possible, in proportion to the project size and scope. The project sponsor initiates the project proposal process, champions the project in the customer organization, and is the ultimate decision-maker for the project. The project sponsor provides support for the Planning engineer, approves major deliverables, and signs off on approvals to proceed to each succeeding project phase. The project sponsor may elect to delegate any of the above responsibilities to other personnel either on or outside the project team.

The project sponsor has ultimate accountability and responsibility for the project and is a member of the steering committee, usually the committee chair (sometimes referred to as the project owner). The sponsor oversees the business management and project management issues that arise outside the formal business of the steering committee. The sponsor also lends support, by advocacy, at senior levels, and ensures that the necessary resources (both financial and human) are available to the project.

The corporate client and project sponsor may be the same person for some projects. The project sponsor is ultimately responsible for ensuring that project benefits are secured before formally closing the project. The project sponsor must be identified for all projects, no matter what the size or complexity.

Customer Organization Management

Customer organization management includes all members of the organization's management team that may exert influence on project team members or be affected by and involved in the development and implementation of the product of the project. The committees that are formed to evaluate and select proposed projects for the customer organization are comprised of members of the customer organization management.

STEERING COMMITTEE

The steering committee is responsible for policy and resourcing decisions essential to the delivery of project outputs and the attainment of project target outcomes. It is also responsible for ensuring appropriate management of the project components outlined in the project business plan, including ultimate accountability for ensuring appropriate risk management processes are applied.

INTERNAL STAKEHOLDERS

Internal stakeholders include all the people that are in any way affected by the new product or service within the customer organization. This may include the project team, the customer organization management, customers who will be affected by the change in customer work practices due to the new product or service. External stakeholders include all the people outside the customer organization that are in any way affected by the new product or service.

CUSTOMER

Customer comprise the business units that identified the need for the product or service the project will develop. Customers can be at all levels of an organization, from commissioner to entry-level clerk.

CUSTOMER REPRESENTATIVES

Customer representatives are members of the customer community that are identified and made available to the project for their subject matter expertise. Their responsibility is to accurately represent their business units' needs to the project team, and to validate the deliverables that describe the product or service that the project will produce.

CONSUMERS

Consumers include all the people that will use the product or service that the project is developing. Consumers internal to the customer organizations may also be customers.

BUSINESS OWNER

The business owner is responsible for managing the project outputs for utilization by the project customers. There may be one or more business owners, at a number of managerial levels, depending on the size of the project. The business owner must be satisfied that the project includes all of the outputs necessary for outcome/benefits realization. The business owner must be identified for all projects, no matter what the size or complexity.

QUALITY CONSULTANT

Large projects generally engage one or more quality consultants to undertake formal quality reviews of the project's processes or outputs. These consultants work independently of the project team, and are often contracted from outside the organization.

PROJECT TEAM

The project team is a group that is responsible for planning and executing the project. It consists of a planning engineer and a variable number of project team members, who are brought in to deliver their tasks according to the project schedule.

The project team is led by the Planning engineer, working for the successful delivery of the project outputs, as outlined in the project execution plan. It is desirable that the project team includes representatives from the business units affected by the project. The composition of the team may change as the project moves through its various phases. The assessment and selection of people with the requisite skills required for each phase of a project is critical to its overall success. The skills should be explicitly identified as a part of the project planning process. The project team is responsible for completing tasks and activities required for delivering project outputs.

PROJECT TEAM MEMBERS

Project team members are responsible for executing tasks and producing deliverables as outlined in the project management plan and directed by the Planning engineer, at whatever level of effort or participation has been defined for them. On larger projects, some project team members may serve as team leaders, providing task and technical leadership.

VENDORS

Vendors are contracted to provide additional products or services the project will require and may be members of the project team.

STEERING COMMITTEE ROLES AND FUNCTIONS

Steering Committee is crucial for the project's success. The important role that Steering Committee members play in a project, both individually and collectively.

The primary function of a Steering Committee is to take responsibility for the business issues associated with a project, including ultimate responsibility for ensuring appropriate risk management processes are applied. Members of a Steering Committee ensure these issues are being adequately addressed and the project remains under control. In practice, these responsibilities involve five main functions:

- Approval of changes to the project and its supporting documentation
- Monitoring and review of the project
- Assistance to the project when required
- Resolution of project conflicts
- Formal acceptance of project deliverables

APPROVAL OF CHANGES TO THE PROJECT

The Steering Committee is responsible for approving major project documentation. Specifically, the Steering Committee approves:

- Prioritization of project objectives and outcomes/benefits
- Budget
- Outputs or deliverables
- Schedule and budget constraints
- Risk minimization strategies
- Project management and quality assurance methodologies

The Steering Committee is also responsible for any major changes to the project. It should be provided with the following information in support of a proposed change:

- Nature and reason for the variation
- Effect of the change
- Revised Project Business Plan, if appropriate
- Suggested actions for the Steering Committee to consider

Changing or emergent issues may require the project scope to be adapted so the project meets the original or modified outcomes/benefits. The Steering Committee is responsible for approving or rejecting these changes to the project and for ensuring that additional resources are provided for incorporating these changes, if required.

MONITORING AND REVIEW OF THE PROJECT

The Steering Committee reviews the status of the project at least at the end of each phase and determines whether the Project Team should progress to the next phase. The review focuses on major project documentation and any variations in the key components, such as outcomes/benefits, risk, costs, returns and output quality.

ASSISTANCE TO THE PROJECT WHEN REQUIRED

The Steering Committee assists the Business Owners and Planning engineer in completing the project by ensuring the project is adequately resourced and has the backing of people with authority. Steering Committee members should be active advocates for the project's outcomes/benefits and help facilitate broad support for it.

RESOLUTION OF PROJECT CONFLICTS

Project conflicts can arise from conflicts in resource allocation, output quality and the level of commitment of project stakeholders and related projects. The Planning engineer is generally the first reference point for the resolution of problems and can solve most internal project problems. Problems arising, which are outside the control of the Planning engineer, are referred to the Project Sponsor or Business Owners for resolution, but there may be occasions when the Steering Committee is asked to help resolve such disputes.

Formal Acceptance of Project Deliverables

Following review and/or acceptance by the Business Owners, the Steering Committee formally reviews and accepts project outputs. Once these deliverables have been accepted by the Steering Committee, any changes must be formally approved. To achieve this function effectively, Steering Committee members must have a broad understanding of project management concepts and the specific approach adopted by the Project Team.

Steering Committee Membership

For Steering Committees to work effectively, the right people must be involved. Steering Committee membership should be based on individual skills and attributes, rather than on their formal roles, and members should maintain membership of a Steering Committee even if their role within the organization changes. However, representatives of important stakeholder groups also should be included.

Steering Committee Meetings

A Steering Committee meets regularly throughout the course of a project to keep track of issues and the progress of the project. The Planning engineer should attend these meetings to be a source of information for Steering Committee members and to be kept informed of Steering Committee decisions. Ideally, the Project Sponsor should chair the Steering Committee meetings.

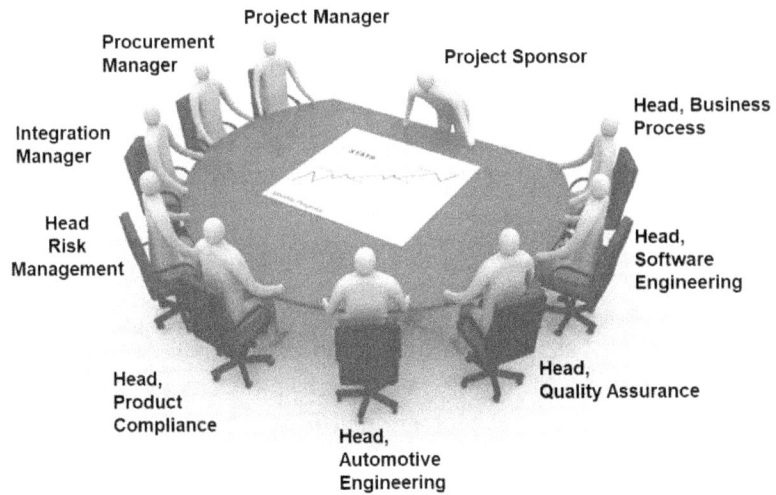

A Steering Committee meeting may cover the following agenda. Introductory items, such as:

- Apologies
- Minutes from last meeting
- Matters arising from minutes
- Project Business Plan issues - amendments, revisions or arising related issues
- Project management issues, including progress reports and consultants' reports
- Important issues at the time of the meeting, such as a budget committee submission, proposed tendering arrangements, sign-off of functional requirements, related projects and so forth
- Review of actions arising from previous Steering Committee meetings - may be useful to keep a formal list of these actions, in order to track them effectively
- Plans for the next meeting

The Steering Committee has responsibility for the project until the project's outcomes/benefits are secured. These outcomes/benefits may not be secured until after the Planning engineer and Team have completed their involvement.

PROJECT MANAGEMENT OFFICE

A project management office (PMO) is a management structure that standardizes the project-related governance processes and facilitates the sharing of resources, methodologies, tools, and techniques. The responsibilities of a PMO can range from providing project management support functions to actually being responsible for the direct management of one or more projects.

There are several types of PMO structures in organizations, each varying in the degree of control and influence they have on projects within the organization, such as:

- **Supportive**. Supportive PMOs provide a consultative role to projects by supplying templates, best practices, training, access to information and lessons learned from other projects. This type of PMO serves as a project repository. The degree of control provided by the PMO is low.

- **Controlling**. Controlling PMOs provide support and require compliance through various means. Compliance may involve adopting project management frameworks or methodologies, using specific templates, forms and tools, or conformance to governance. The degree of control provided by the PMO is moderate.

- **Directive**. Directive PMOs take control of the projects by directly managing the projects. The degree of control provided by the PMO is high.

A primary function of a PMO is to support Planning engineers in a variety of ways which may include, but are not limited to:

- Managing shared resources across all projects administered by the PMO;
- Identifying and developing project management methodology, best practices, and standards;
- Coaching, mentoring, training, and oversight;
- Monitoring compliance with project management standards, policies, procedures, and templates by means of project audits;
- Developing and managing project policies, procedures, templates, and other shared documentation (organizational process assets); and
- Coordinating communication across projects.

The key ingredients to project management are people, processes, and technology. Technology is a tool, while processes provide a structure and path for managing and carrying out the project. The success of a project, however, is often determined by the various project stakeholders, as well as who is (or who is not) on the project team. In this chapter, we will discuss the human resources of project management. The area of project human resource management entails:

- organizational planning
- staff acquisition
- team development.

Organization planning focuses on the roles, responsibilities, and relationships among the project stakeholders. These individuals or groups can be internal or external to the project.

Moreover, organizational planning involves creating a project structure that will support the project processes and stakeholders so that the project is carried out efficiently and effectively.

Staff acquisition includes staffing the project with the best available human resources. Effective staffing involves having policies, procedures, and practices to guide the recruitment of appropriately skilled and experienced staff. Moreover, it may include negotiating for staff from other functional areas within the organization.

Team development involves creating an environment to develop and support the individual team members and the team itself.

This chapter will expand upon these three subjects and integrate several relatively recent concepts for understanding the governance structure in project management. Three primary organizational structure: the functional, project, and matrix will be described. In addition, the various opportunities and challenges for projects conducted under each structure will be discussed. As a project manager or project team member, it is important to understand an organization's structure since this will determine authorities, roles, responsibilities, communication channels, and availability of resources.

Once the project team is in place, it is important that the project team learn from each other and from past project experiences. Thus, the idea of learning cycles will be introduced as a tool for team learning and for capturing lessons learned that can be documented, stored, and retrieved using a knowledge management system

PROJECT STAKEHOLDERS

Stakeholders are individuals, groups, or even organizations that have a stake, or claim, in the project's outcome. Often, we think of stakeholders as only those individuals or groups having an interest in the successful outcome of a project, but the sad truth is that there are many who can gain from a project's failure. While the formal organization tells us a little about the stakeholders and what their interests may be, the informal organization paints a much more interesting picture.

Types of Stakeholders in Project Management

Diagram showing STAKEHOLDERS at the center with arrows pointing to: CUSTOMERS, SUPPLIERS, GOVERNMENT, LENDERS, DIRECTORS, EMPLOYEES, SHAREHOLDERS, PUBLIC.

PROJECT MANAGER

One of the most critical decisions in project management is selecting a project manager or team leader. The project manager is usually assigned to the project at the earliest stages of the project life cycle, but a new one may be brought in as replacement in the later stages of a project. The project manager must play many roles. First, the project manager must play a managerial role that focuses on planning, organizing, and controlling. The project manager, for example, is responsible for developing the project plan, organizing the project resources, and then overseeing execution of the plan. The project manager must also perform many administrative functions, including performance reviews, project tracking and reporting, and other general day-to-day responsibilities.

The success of the project, of course, depends not only on the project team, but also on the contributions and support of all project stakeholders as well. Therefore, the project manager must build and nurture the relationships among the various stakeholders. To do this effectively, the project manager must play a strong leadership role. While the managerial role focuses on planning, organizing, and controlling, leadership focuses on getting people motivated and then headed down the right path towards a common goal.

Choosing a project manager for a project is analogous to hiring an employee. It is important to look at his or her background, knowledge, skill sets, and overall strengths and weaknesses. Some attributes of a successful project manager include:

ABILITY TO COMMUNICATE WITH PEOPLE

A project manager must have strong communication skills. A project manager need not to be a great motivational speaker, but should have the ability to connect with people, share a common vision, and get everyone to respond or head in the right direction.

ABILITY TO DEAL WITH PEOPLE

Aside from being a good communicator, a project manager must have the soft skills for dealing with people, their egos, and their agendas. The project manager must be a good listener, hearing what people say and understanding what they mean. This skill allows the project manager to get below the surface of issues when people are not being completely honest or open without being annoying or alienating them.

ABILITY TO CREATE AND SUSTAIN RELATIONSHIPS

A good project manager must be able to build bridges instead of walls. Acting as a peacemaker or negotiator among the project client or sponsor, top management, the project team, customers, suppliers, vendors, subcontractors, and so forth may be necessary.

ABILITY TO ORGANIZE

A project manager must be good at organizing developing the project plan, acquiring resources, and creating an effective project environment. The project manager must also know and understand both the details and the big picture, which requires a familiarity with the details of the project plan and also an understanding of how contingencies may impact the plan.

The following list of project roles gives an indication of the type of accountabilities, responsibilities and tasks generally allocated to those people involved in a project. As projects vary, including in size and complexity, the roles required, and even the tasks and responsibilities within those roles, will vary. The information below provides a starting point, which should be discussed with the appropriate groups or persons nominated to fill positions in a project's governance structure, with the agreed breakdown of accountabilities and responsibilities documented for large and/or complex projects. The most crucial issue is to have clearly assigned roles and transparency of the project governance structure.

However, all projects must have, as a minimum, the roles of Project Sponsor, Business Owner(s) and Project Manager within the governance structure (though not necessarily different person). That is:

- A person responsible and accountable for the project output and securing its benefits (Project Sponsor)

- A person who will manage the project outputs after project closure, and is accountable for realization of the benefits (Business Owners)
- A person who will manage the project and deliver the outputs (Project Manager)

BUDGET MANAGEMENT

Project Manager must be capable to prepare the project budget. All businesses have a responsibility to the monies they are allotted, have earned, and have acquired through donations. In project management, the work completed within a project must be measured for value and accounted for. The budget the organization has set for the project must be guarded. Ultimately, the success of the project should generate an increase in funds, productivity, or efficiency for the sponsoring organization.

PROJECT RESOURCES

Project Manager must be organized. How much time has been wasted looking for documentation, contracts, or permits? How much money has been lost due to disorganization? How many projects have failed because the project manager did not keep and maintain accurate records? Organization is a methodical approach to storing and retrieving information, as it is needed. Organization does not require a spotless desk, thousands of labelled file folders, or archives of every project-related document. Organization requires thorough, fast, and reliable access to project data.

PROJECT SPONSOR

The project sponsor is a manager with demonstrable interest in the outcome of the project who is responsible for securing spending authority and resources for the project. Ideally, the project sponsor should be the highest-ranking manager possible, in proportion to the project size and scope. The project sponsor initiates the project proposal process, champions the project in the customer organization, and is the ultimate decision-maker for the project. The project sponsor provides support for the project manager, approves major deliverables, and signs off on approvals to proceed to each succeeding project phase. The project sponsor may elect to delegate any of the above responsibilities to other personnel either on or outside the project team.

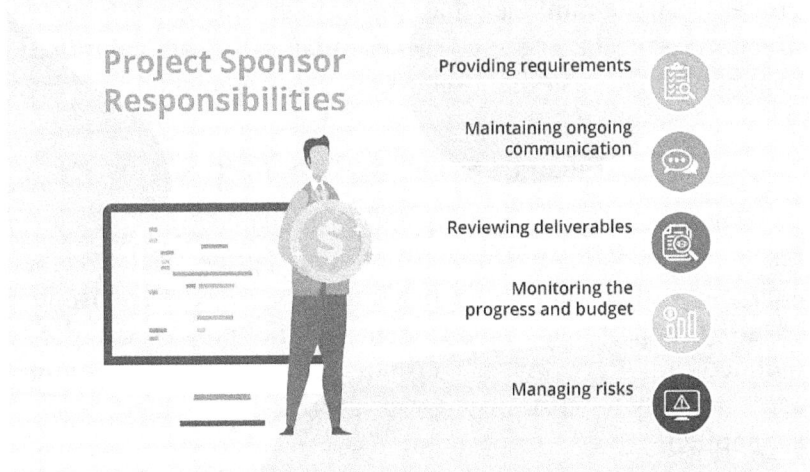

The project sponsor has ultimate accountability and responsibility for the project and is a member of the steering committee, usually the committee chair (sometimes referred to as project owner). The sponsor oversees the business management and project management issues that arise outside the formal business of the steering committee. The sponsor also lends support, by advocacy, at senior levels, and ensures that the necessary resources (both financial and human) are available to the project.

The corporate client and project sponsor may be the same person for some projects. The project sponsor is ultimately responsible for ensuring that project benefits are secured before formally closing the project. The project sponsor must be identified for all projects, no matter what the size or complexity.

CUSTOMER ORGANIZATION MANAGEMENT

Customer organization management (pom) includes all members of the organization's management team that may exert influence on project team members or be affected by and involved in the development and implementation of the product of the project. The committees that are formed to evaluate and select proposed projects for the customer organization are comprised of members of the customer organization management.

PROJECT STEERING COMMITTEE

The steering committee is responsible for policy and resourcing decisions essential to delivery of project outputs and the attainment of project target outcomes. It is also responsible for ensuring appropriate management of the project components outlined in the project business plan, including ultimate accountability for ensuring appropriate risk management processes are applied.

PROJECT STAKEHOLDERS

Internal stakeholders include all the people that are in any way affected by the new product or service within the customer organization. This may include the project team, the customer organization management, customers who will be affected by the change in customer work practices due to the new product or service. External stakeholders include all the people outside the customer organization that are in any way affected by the new product or service.

CUSTOMER

Customer comprise the business units that identified the need for the product or service the project will develop. Customers can be at all levels of an organization, from commissioner to entry-level clerk.

CUSTOMER REPRESENTATIVES

Customer representatives are members of the customer community that are identified and made available to the project for their subject matter expertise. Their responsibility is to accurately represent their business units' needs to the project team, and to validate the deliverables that describe the product or service that the project will produce.

CONSUMERS

Consumers include all the people that will use the product or service that the project is developing. Consumers internal to the customer organizations may also be customers.

BUSINESS OWNER

The business owner is responsible for managing the project outputs for utilization by the project customers. There may be one or more business owners, at a number of managerial levels, depending on the size of the project. The business owner must be satisfied that the project includes all of the outputs necessary for outcome/benefits realization. The business owner must be identified for all projects, no matter what the size or complexity.

Quality Consultant

Large projects generally engage one or more quality consultants to undertake formal quality reviews of the project's processes or outputs. These consultants work independently of the project team, and are often contracted from outside the organization.

Project Manager

The project manager is the person who is responsible for ensuring that the project team completes the project. The project manager develops the project plan with the team and manages the team's performance of project tasks. It is also the responsibility of the project manager to secure acceptance and approval of deliverables from the project sponsor and stakeholders.

The project manager is contracted by the project sponsor and steering committee to deliver the defined project outputs. They are responsible for organizing the project into one or more sub-projects, managing the day-to-day aspects of the project, developing the project management plan, resolving planning and implementation issues, and monitoring progress and budget.

The project manager will:

- develop and maintain a project management plan
- manage and monitor the project activity through detailed plans and schedules
- report to the project sponsor and steering committee at regular intervals
- manage (client/provider/stakeholder) expectations through formal specification and agreement of goals, objectives, scope, outputs, resources required, budget, schedule, project structure, roles and responsibilities.

It is essential that the project manager has high-level project management skills. A project manager cannot lead effectively unless they have credibility. For most projects, it means the project manager must have knowledge of how the outputs will be created and how they will achieve the outcomes or benefits. The project manager must be identified for all projects, no matter what the size or complexity.

PROJECT TEAM

The project team is a group that is responsible for planning and executing the project. It consists of a project manager and a variable number of project team members, who are brought in to deliver their tasks according to the project schedule.

The project team is led by the project manager, working for the successful delivery of the project outputs, as outlined in the project execution plan. It is desirable that the project team includes representatives from the business units affected by the project. The composition of the team may change as the project moves through its various phases. The assessment and selection of people with the requisite skills required for each phase of a project is critical to its overall success. The skills should be explicitly identified as a part of the project planning process. The project team is responsible for completing tasks and activities required for delivering project outputs.

PROJECT TEAM MEMBERS

Project team members are responsible for executing tasks and producing deliverables as outlined in the project management plan and directed by the project manager, at whatever level of effort or participation has been defined for them.

On larger projects, some project team members may serve as team leaders, providing task and technical leadership.

CONSULTANTS

Consultants are employed from outside the organization to provide specialist or other expertise unavailable from internal resources. Typically, project consultants may include:

- engineering specialists who define and manage the technological aspects of the project
- representatives employed by stakeholders to ensure their interests are represented and managed
- legal advisers who assist in the development and review of the contractual documentation

CONTRACTORS

Contractors also may be engaged to work as part of the project team. Contractors are employed, external to the business area, to provide a specified service in relation to the development of project outputs.

Examples include:

- prepare and deliver training to staff in the business area
- develop and deliver marketing programs
- develop guides and/or manuals
- develop business application software

VENDORS

Vendors are contracted to provide additional products or services the project will require and may be members of the project team.

PROJECT STEERING COMMITTEE

Steering Committee is crucial for the project's success. The important role that Steering Committee members play in a project, both individually and collectively.

The primary function of a Steering Committee is to take responsibility for the business issues associated with a project, including ultimate responsibility for ensuring appropriate risk management processes are applied. Members of a Steering Committee ensure these issues are being adequately addressed and the project remains under control. In practice, these responsibilities involve five main functions:

- Approval of changes to the project and its supporting documentation
- Monitoring and review of the project
- Assistance to the project when required
- Resolution of project conflicts
- Formal acceptance of project deliverables

The Steering Committee is responsible for approving major project documentation. Specifically, the Steering Committee approves:

- Prioritization of project objectives and outcomes/benefits
- Budget
- Outputs or deliverables
- Schedule and budget constraints
- Risk minimization strategies
- Project management and quality assurance methodologies

The Steering Committee is also responsible for any major changes to the project. It should be provided with the following information in support of a proposed change:

- Nature and reason for the variation
- Effect of the change
- Revised Project Business Plan, if appropriate
- Suggested actions for the Steering Committee to consider

Changing or emergent issues may require the project scope to be adapted so the project meets the original or modified outcomes/benefits. The Steering Committee is responsible for approving or rejecting these changes to the project and for ensuring that additional resources are provided for incorporating these changes, if required.

MONITORING AND REVIEW

The Steering Committee reviews the status of the project at least at the end of each phase and determines whether the Project Team should progress to the next phase. The review focuses on major project documentation and any variations in the key components, such as outcomes/benefits, risk, costs, returns and output quality.

ASSISTANCE TO THE PROJECT

The Steering Committee assists the Business Owners and Project Manager in completing the project by ensuring the project is adequately resourced and has the backing of people with authority. Steering Committee members should be active advocates for the project's outcomes/benefits and help facilitate broad support for it.

RESOLUTION OF PROJECT CONFLICTS

Project conflicts can arise from conflicts in resource allocation, output quality and the level of commitment of project stakeholders and related projects.

The Project Manager is generally the first reference point for the resolution of problems and can solve most internal project problems. Problems arising, which are outside the control of the Project Manager, are referred to the Project Sponsor or Business Owners for resolution, but there may be occasions when the Steering Committee is asked to help resolve such disputes.

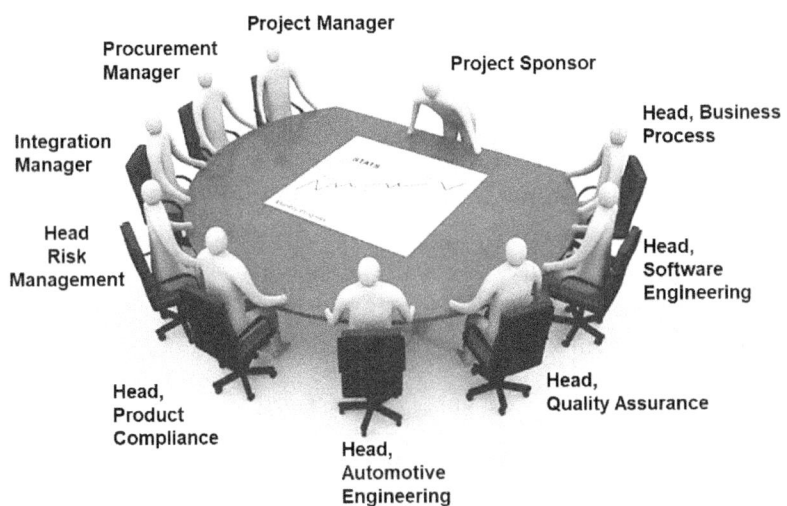

Formal Acceptance of Project Deliverables

Following review and/or acceptance by the Business Owners, the Steering Committee formally reviews and accepts project outputs. Once these deliverables have been accepted by the Steering Committee, any changes must be formally approved. To achieve this function effectively, Steering Committee members must have a broad understanding of project management concepts and the specific approach adopted by the Project Team.

Steering Committee Membership

For Steering Committees to work effectively, the right people must be involved. Steering Committee membership should be based on individual skills and attributes, rather than on their formal roles, and members should maintain membership of a Steering Committee even if their role within the organization changes. However, representatives of important stakeholder groups also should be included.

Steering Committee Meetings

A Steering Committee meets regularly throughout the course of a project to keep track of issues and the progress of the project. The Project Manager should attend these meetings to be a source of information for Steering Committee members and to be kept informed of Steering Committee decisions. Ideally, the Project Sponsor should chair the Steering Committee meetings. A Steering Committee meeting may cover the following agenda:

- Apologies
- Minutes from last meeting
- Matters arising from minutes
- Project Business Plan issues - amendments, revisions or arising related issues
- Project management issues, including progress reports and consultants' reports
- Important issues at the time of the meeting, such as a budget committee submission, proposed tendering arrangements, sign-off of functional requirements, related projects and so forth

- Review of actions arising from previous Steering Committee meetings - may be useful to keep a formal list of these actions, in order to track them effectively
- Plans for the next meeting

The Steering Committee has responsibility for the project until the project's outcomes/benefits are secured. These outcomes/benefits may not be secured until after the Project Manager and Team have completed their involvement.

PROJECT MANAGEMENT OFFICE

A project management office (PMO) is a management structure that standardizes the project-related governance processes and facilitates the sharing of resources, methodologies, tools, and techniques. The responsibilities of a PMO can range from providing project management support functions to actually being responsible for the direct management of one or more projects.

There are several types of PMO structures in organizations, each varying in the degree of control and influence they have on projects within the organization, such as:

- **Supportive.** Supportive PMOs provide a consultative role to projects by supplying templates, best practices, training, access to information and lessons learned from other projects. This type of PMO serves as a project repository. The degree of control provided by the PMO is low.

- **Controlling**. Controlling PMOs provide support and require compliance through various means. Compliance may involve adopting project management frameworks or methodologies, using specific templates, forms and tools, or conformance to governance. The degree of control provided by the PMO is moderate.

- **Directive**. Directive PMOs take control of the projects by directly managing the projects. The degree of control provided by the PMO is high.

A primary function of a PMO is to support project managers in a variety of ways which may include, but are not limited to:

- Managing shared resources across all projects administered by the PMO;
- Identifying and developing project management methodology, best practices, and standards;
- Coaching, mentoring, training, and oversight;
- Monitoring compliance with project management standards, policies, procedures, and templates by means of project audits;
- Developing and managing project policies, procedures, templates, and other shared documentation (organizational process assets); and
- Coordinating communication across projects.

Chapter 10 : PLAN QUALITY ASSURANCE

Quality assurance (QA) is any systematic process of determining whether a product or service meets specified requirements. QA establishes and maintains set requirements for developing or manufacturing reliable products. A quality assurance system is meant to increase customer confidence and a company's credibility, while also improving work processes and efficiency, and it enables a company to better compete with others.

The ISO (International Organization for Standardization) is a driving force behind QA practices and mapping the processes used to implement QA. QA is often paired with the ISO 9000 international standard. Many companies use ISO 9000 to ensure that their quality assurance system is in place and effective.

The concept of QA as a formalized practice started in the manufacturing industry, and it has since spread to most industries, including software development.

IMPORTANCE OF QUALITY ASSURANCE

Quality assurance helps a company create products and services that meet the needs, expectations, and requirements of customers. It yields high-quality product offerings that build trust and loyalty with customers. The standards and procedures defined by a quality assurance program help prevent product defects before they arise

The project manager communicates with the Customer to establish and document all quality activities to be implemented during the project to ensure the defined quality standards will be met. This is called quality assurance. Sometimes quality assurance for specific types of deliverables is performed by a separate Quality Assurance team. If an organization does not have the luxury of a Quality Assurance team, the required activities will need to be performed by designated Project Team members or Customers.

Examples of quality assurance activities include:

- Collecting project documentation
- Conducting audits
- Verifying business requirements
- Performing testing activities

A description of all quality activities to be implemented during the course of the project should be included in the project Quality Management Plan.

QUALITY ASSURANCE METHODS

Quality assurance utilizes one of three methods:

- Failure testing, which continually tests a product to determine if it breaks or fails. For physical products that need to withstand stress, this could involve testing the product under heat, pressure, or vibration. For software products, failure testing might involve placing the software under high usage or load conditions.

- Statistical process control (SPC), a methodology based on objective data and analysis and developed by Walter Shewhart at Western Electric Company and Bell Telephone Laboratories in the 1920s and 1930s. This methodology uses statistical methods to manage and control the production of products.

- Total quality management (TQM), which applies quantitative methods as the basis for continuous improvement. TQM relies on facts, data and analysis to support product planning and performance reviews.

QA VERSUS QC

Some people may confuse the term quality assurance with quality control (QC). Although the two concepts share similarities, there are important distinctions between them. In effect, QA provides the overall guidelines used anywhere, and QC is a production-focused process for things such as inspections. QA is any systematic process for making sure a product meets specified requirements, whereas QC addresses other issues, such as individual inspections or defects.

In terms of software development, QA practices seek to prevent malfunctioning code or products, while QC implements testing and troubleshooting and fixes code.

QA Standards

QA standards have changed and been updated over time, and ISO standards need to change in order to stay relevant to today's businesses. The latest in the ISO 9000 series is ISO 9001:2015. The guidance in ISO 9001:2015 includes a stronger customer focus, top management practices and how they can change a company, and keeping pace with continuing improvements. Along with general improvements to ISO 9001, ISO 9001:2015 includes improvements to its structure and more information for risk-based decision-making.

Quality Assurance In Software

Software quality assurance (SQA) systematically finds patterns and the actions needed to improve development cycles. Finding and fixing coding errors can carry unintended consequences; it is possible to fix one thing, yet break other features and functionality at the same time. SQA has become important for developers as a means of avoiding errors before they occur, saving development time and expenses. Even with SQA processes in place, an update to software can break other features and cause defects commonly known as bugs.

There have been numerous SQA strategies. For example, Capability Maturity Model Integration (CMMI) is a performance improvement-focused SQA model. CMMI works by ranking maturity levels of areas within an organization, and it identifies optimizations that can be used for improvement. Rank levels range from being disorganized to being fully optimal.

Software development methodologies have developed over time that relies on SQA, such as Waterfall, Agile, and Scrum. Each development process seeks to optimize work efficiency.

- Waterfall is the traditional linear approach to software development. It's a step-by-step process that typically involves gathering requirements, formalizing a design, implementing code, code testing and remediation and release. It is often seen as too slow, which is why alternative development methods were constructed.
- Agile is a team-oriented software development methodology where each step in the work process is approached as a sprint. Agile software development is highly adaptive, but it is less predictive because the scope of the project can easily change.
- Scrum is a combination of both processes where developers are split into teams to handle specific tasks, and each task is separated into multiple sprints.

To implement a QA system, first set goals for the standard. Consider the advantages and tradeoffs of each approach, such as maximizing efficacy, reducing cost, or minimizing errors. Management must be willing to implement process changes and work together to support the QA system and establish standards for quality.

QA Team

A portion of careers in SQA includes job options like SQA engineers, SQA Analysts and SQA test automation. SQA engineers monitor and test software through development. An SQA Analyst will monitor the implication and practices of SQA over software development cycles. SQA test automation requires the individual to create programs to automate the SQA process.

These programs compare predicted outcomes with actual outcomes. This work is used for constant testing.

SQA Tools

Software testing is an integral part of software quality assurance. Testing saves time, effort and cost, and it enables a quality end product to be optimally produced. There are numerous software tools and platforms that developers can employ to automate and orchestrate testing in order to facilitate SQA goals. Selenium is an open-source software testing program that can run tests in a variety of popular software languages, such as C#, Java, and Python.

Another open-source program, called Jenkins, enables developers and QA staff to run and test code in real-time. It's well-suited for a fast-paced environment because it automates tasks related to the building and testing of software.

For web apps or application program interfaces (APIs), Postman will automate and run tests. It is available for Mac, Windows, and Linux, and it can support Swagger and RAML formatting.

QA Uses By Industry

The following are a few examples of quality assurance in use by industries:

- Manufacturing, the industry that formalized the quality assurance discipline. Manufacturers need to ensure that assembled products are created without defects and meet the defined product specifications and requirements.

- Food production, which uses X-ray systems, among other techniques, to detect physical contaminants in the food production process. The X-ray systems ensure that contaminants are removed and eliminated before products leave the factory.

- Pharmaceutical employs different quality assurance approaches during each stage of a drug's development. Across the different stages, the QA processes include reviewing documents, approving equipment calibration, reviewing training records, reviewing manufacturing records and investigating market returns.

QA vs. Testing

QA is different from testing. QA is more focused on processes and procedures, while testing is focused on the logistics of using a product in order to find defects. QA defines the standards around testing to ensure that a product meets defined business requirements. Testing involves the more tactical process of validating the function of a product and identifying issues.

Pros and Cons of QA

The quality of products and services is a key competitive differentiator. Quality assurance helps ensure that organizations create and ship products that are clear of defects and meet the needs and expectations of customers. High-quality products result in satisfied customers, which can result in customer loyalty, repeat purchases, upsell, and advocacy.

Quality assurance can lead to cost reductions stemming from the prevention of product defects. If a product is shipped to customers and a defect is discovered, an organization incurs costs in customer support, such as receiving the defect report and troubleshooting. It also acquires the cost of addressing the defect, such as service or engineering hours to correct it, testing to validate the fix and cost to ship the updated product to the market.

QA does require a substantial investment in people and processes. People must define a process workflow and oversee its implementation by members of a QA team. This can be a time-consuming process that impacts the delivery date of products. With few exceptions, the disadvantage of QA is more a requirement, a necessary step that must be undertaken to ship a quality product. Without QA, more serious disadvantages arise, such as product bugs and the market's dissatisfaction or rejection of the product.

Chapter 11 : PROJECT QUALITY MANAGEMENT

PROJECT QUALITY MANAGEMENT

Quality management is the process of ensuring that all project activities necessary to design, plan and implement a project are effective and efficient concerning the purpose of the objective and its performance. Project Quality Management (PQM) is not a separate, independent process that occurs at the end of an activity to measure the level of quality of the output. It is not purchasing the most expensive material or services available on the market. Quality and grade are not the same. Grades are characteristics of a material or service such as additional features. A product may be of good quality (no defects) and be of low grade (few or no extra features).

Quality management is a continuous process that starts and ends with the project. It is more about preventing and avoiding than measuring and fixing poor-quality outputs. It is part of every project management process from the moment the project initiates to the final steps in the project closure phase.

Quality Management focuses on improving stakeholder satisfaction through continuous and incremental improvements to processes, including removing unnecessary activities; it achieves that by the continuous improvement of the quality of material and services provided to the key project stakeholders. It is not about finding and fixing errors after the fact, quality management is the continuous monitoring and application of quality processes in all aspects of the project.

- PQM uses policies and procedures to implement the organization's quality management system and, as appropriate, it supports continuous process improvement activities as undertaken on behalf of the performing organization.

- PQM works to ensure that the project requirements, including product requirements, are met and validated.
- PQM Implement quality management which includes quality planning, quality assurance, quality control.
- PQM address both the quality management of the project and the quality of the product or service of the project.

DEFINITION OF QUALITY

Quality is defined as "the totality of characteristics of an entity that bear on its ability to satisfy stated or implied needs. The stated and implied quality needs are the inputs used in defining project requirements from the project sponsor and the key project stakeholders. It is also defined as the "Conformance to requirements or fitness for use" which means that the product or services must meet the intended objectives of the project and have value to the project sponsor and key project stakeholders and that the key project stakeholders can use the material or service as it was originally intended. The central focus of quality management is meeting or exceeding stakeholders' expectations and conforming to the project design and specifications.

The ultimate judge for quality is the beneficiary or the customer representatives of the performing organization who are the "key stakeholders", and represents how close the project outputs and deliverables come to meeting the key project stakeholders' requirements and expectations. How a beneficiary defines quality may be completely subjective, but there are many ways to make quality objective; by defining the individual characteristics and determining one or more metrics that can be collected to mirror the characteristic. For instance, one of the features of a quality product may be that it has a minimum number of errors. This characteristic can be measured by counting errors and defects after the product is used.

Quality management is not an event, it is a process, a consistently high-quality product or service cannot be produced by a defective process. Quality management is a repetitive cycle of measuring quality, and updating processes until the desired quality is achieved.

PROJECT QUALITY MANAGEMENT PROCESSES

The main principle of project quality management is to ensure the project will meet or exceed stakeholders' needs and expectations. The project team must develop a good relationship with key stakeholders, especially the project sponsor and the key project stakeholders of the project, to understand what quality means to them. One of the causes for poor project evaluations is the project focuses only on meeting the written requirements for the main outputs and ignores other stakeholder needs and expectations for the project.

Quality must be viewed on an equal level with scope, schedule, and budget. If a project sponsor is not satisfied with the quality of how the project is delivering the outcomes, the project team will need to make adjustments to the scope, schedule, and budget to satisfy the project sponsor's needs and expectations. To deliver the project scope on time and within budget is not enough; to achieve stakeholder satisfaction the project must develop a good working relationship with all stakeholders and understand their stated or implied needs.

Project Quality Management consists of three main processes with reference to PMBOK® body of knowledge:

PLAN QUALITY MANAGEMENT

Plan Quality Management refers to the process of identifying quality requirements and standards for the project and its deliverables and documenting how the project will demonstrate compliance with quality requirements.

Perform Quality Assurance

Perform Quality Assurance refers to the process of auditing the quality requirements and the results from quality control measurements to ensure that appropriate quality standards and operational definitions are used.

Project Manager communicates with the Customer to establish and document all quality activities to be implemented during the course of the project to ensure the defined quality standards will be met. This is called quality assurance. Sometimes quality assurance for specific types of deliverables is performed by a separate Quality Assurance Department. If an organization does not have the luxury of a Quality Assurance Department, the required activities will need to be performed by designated Project Team members or Customers.

Examples of quality assurance activities include:

- Collecting project documentation
- Conducting audits
- Verifying business requirements
- Performing testing

A description of all quality activities to be implemented during the course of the project should be included in the Quality Management Plan.

Control Quality

Control Quality refers to the process of monitoring and recording results of executing quality activities to assess performance and recommend necessary changes.

Plan Quality Management

The first step in the plan quality management process is to define quality. The Project Engineer and the team must identify what quality standards will be used in the project, it will look at the project sponsor, key project stakeholders, the organization and other key stakeholders to come up with a good definition of quality. In some instances, the organization or the area of specialization of the project (engineering, IT, construction, health, water, or education) may have some standard definitions of quality that can be used by the project.

Identifying quality standards is a key component of quality definition that will help identify the key characteristics that will govern project activities and ensure the key project stakeholders and project sponsors will accept the project outcomes.

Quality management implies the ability to anticipate situations and prepare actions that will help bring the desired outcomes. The goal is the prevention of defects through the creation of actions that will ensure that the project team understands what is defined as quality.

Sources of Quality Definition

One source for the definition of quality comes from the project sponsor. The project must establish conversations with the project sponsor to be familiar with and come to a common understanding of what the project sponsor defines as quality. The project sponsor may have certain standards of what is expected from the project, and how the project delivers the expected benefits to the key project stakeholders. This is in line with the project's ultimate objective that the project outcomes have the ability to satisfy the stated or implied needs.

Another source for quality definition comes from the key project stakeholders; the project team must be able to understand how the key project stakeholders define quality from their perspective, a perspective that is more focused on fitness for use, the project outcomes must be relevant to the current needs of the key project stakeholders and must result in improvements to their lives. The team can create, as part of the baseline data collection, questions that seek to understand how the key project stakeholders define the project will meet their needs and a question that also helps define what project success looks like from the perspective of a beneficiary.

The development organization may have its own quality standards that can reflect the technical and managerial nature of the project. The organization may require from the project timely and accurate delivery of project information needed for decision-making, or compliance to international or locally recognized quality standards that define specific technical areas of the project, this is quite often in health, water and nutrition projects.

QUALITY CHARACTERISTICS

All materials or services have characteristics that facilitate the identification of its quality. The characteristics are part of the conditions of how the material, equipment and services are able to meet the requirements of the project and are fit for use by the key project stakeholders. Quality characteristics relate to the attributes, measures and methods attached to that particular product or service.

- **Functionality** is the degree, by which equipment performs its intended function, this is important especially for clinical equipment, that the operation should behave as expected.

- **Performance** is how well a product or service performs the key project stakeholders intended use. A water system should be designed to support extreme conditions and require little maintenance to reduce the cost to the community and increase its sustainability.

- **Reliability** represents the ability of the service or product to perform as intended under normal conditions without unacceptable failures. The material used for blood testing should be able to provide the information consistently and dependably that will help identify critical diseases. The trust of the key project stakeholders is dependent upon the quality of the tests.

- **Relevance** represents the characteristic of how a product or service meets the actual needs of the key project stakeholders, it should be pertinent, applicable, and appropriate to its intended use or application.

- **Timeliness** represents how the product or service is delivered in time to solve the problems when its needed and not after, this is a crucial characteristic for health and emergency relief work.

- **Suitability** defines the fitness of its use, it's appropriateness and correctness, the agriculture equipment must be designed to operate on the soul conditions the key project stakeholders will use it on.

- **Completeness** defines the quality that the service is to be completed and includes all the entire scope of services. Training sessions should be completed and include all the material needed to build a desired skill or knowledge.

- **Consistency** ensures services are delivered in the same way for every beneficiary. For example, clinical tests need to be done using the same procedure for every patient.

Does the product or service meet its intended purpose?

Machine is useless if the suction module failed to function

Quality characteristics are not limited to the material, equipment or service delivered to the key project stakeholders, but also apply to the material, equipment, and services the project staff uses to deliver the project outputs. These include the vehicles, computers, various equipment, and tools and consulting services the project purchases and uses to carry out its activities.

Quality characteristics must be included in all materials, equipment and services the project will purchase, the procurement officers must have a complete description of what is required by the project, otherwise, a procurement office may purchase the goods or services based on her or his information of the product.

What went wrong - A project requested the purchase of 1000 tents for a community displaced by floods, the purchase request had no specifications for its intended use (suitability), and resistance (performance). The procurement officer only knew that the tents were needed as soon as possible (timeliness), so he purchased, based on his knowledge of what a tent looks like, 1000 camping tents, they were delivered to the refugee camps on the requested timeframe, and the Project Engineer was happy. But the next day all families that received the tents were complaining that they were not good for the cold nights and too small to accommodate their extended families. The project purchased the tents under budget and within the specified timeframe but the key project stakeholders rejected them because they did not meet their needs (quality services are poor).

WHAT IS A QUALITY PLAN?

A Quality Plan is a document, or several documents, that together specify quality standards, practices, resources, specifications, and the sequence of activities relevant to a particular product, service, project, or contract. Quality Plan should define:

- Objectives to be attained (for example, characteristics or specifications, uniformity, effectiveness, aesthetics, cycle time, cost, natural resources, utilization, yield, dependability, and so on).
- Steps in the processes that constitute the operating practice or procedures of the organization.
- Allocation of responsibilities, authority, and resources during the different phases of the process or project.
- Specific documented standards, practices, procedures, and instructions to be applied.
- Suitable testing, inspection, examination, and audit programs at appropriate stages.
- A documented procedure for changes and modifications to a quality plan as a process is improved.
- A method for measuring the achievement of quality objectives.
- Other actions necessary to meet the objectives.

At the highest level, quality goals and plans should be integrated with the overall strategic plans of the organization. As organizational objectives and plans are deployed throughout the organization, each function fashions its own best way of contributing to the top-level goals and objectives.

At lower levels, the quality plan assumes the role of an actionable plan. Such plans may take many different forms depending on the outcome they are to produce. Quality plans may also be represented by more than one type of document to produce a given outcome.

QUALITY MANAGEMENT PLAN

Part of defining quality involves developing a quality management plan and a quality checklist that will be used during the project implementation phase. This checklist will ensure the project team and other actors are delivering the project outputs according to the quality requirements.

Once the project has defined the quality standards and quality characteristics, it will create a project quality plan that describes all the quality definitions and standards relevant to the project, it will highlight the standards that must be followed to comply with regulatory requirements set up by the project sponsor, the organization and external agencies such as the local government and professional organizations (health, nutrition, etc.)

The quality plan also describes the conditions that the services and materials must possess in order to satisfy the needs and expectations of the project stakeholders, it describes the situations or conditions that make an output fall below quality standards, this information is used to gain a common understanding among the project team to help them identify what is above and what is below a quality standard.

The quality plan also includes the procedure to ensure that the quality standards are being followed by all project staff. The plan also includes the steps required to monitor and control quality and the approval process to make changes to the quality standards and the quality plan.

EXAMPLE OF A QUALITY PLAN

Let's take a look at a manufacturing company that machines metal parts. Its quality plan consists of applicable procedures that include describing the production process and responsibilities, applicable workmanship standards, the measurement tolerances acceptable, the description of the material standards, and so forth. These may all be separate documents.

Deliverable	Quality Event	Quality Materials	Purpose
Preliminary Business Case	Expert Review	Template for Business Case Approved Business Case for Project ABC	Ensure the information is accurate and well constructed prior to submission to Steering Committee
Final Business Case	Formal Inspection by Sponsor	Template for Business Case	Ensure the Business Case is in a fit state to be submitted to the Finance Review Committee
Project Definition	Walk-through of early draft	Template for Project Definition	Review early draft for completeness
	Peer Review of final draft		Review final draft for completeness and construction
Database Design	Expert Review of physical model	Standard for Database Design	Compliance with standard General accuracy

More variable information that pertains to a particular customer may be spelled out on individual work orders. Work orders specify the machine setups and tolerances, operations to be performed, tests, inspections, handling, storing, packaging, and delivery steps to be followed.

An operating-level quality plan translates the customer requirements into actions required to produce the desired outcome and couples this with applicable procedures, standards, practices, and protocols to specify precisely what is needed, who will do it, and how it will be done. A quality control plan may specify product tolerances, testing parameters, and acceptance criteria. While the terminology may differ, the basic approach is similar for service and other types of organizations.

QUALITY ASSURANCE

Assurance is the activity of providing evidence to create confidence among all stakeholders that the quality-related activities are being performed effectively; and that all planned actions are being done to provide adequate confidence that a product or service will satisfy the stated requirements for quality.

Quality Assurance is a process to provide confirmation based on evidence to ensure to the project sponsor, key project stakeholders, organization management, and other stakeholders that the product meet needs, expectations, and other requirements. It assures the existence and effectiveness of process and procedures tools, and safeguards are in place to make sure that the expected levels of quality will be reached to produce quality outputs.

Quality assurance occurs during the implementation phase of the project and includes the evaluation of the overall performance of the project on a regular basis to provide confidence that the project will satisfy the quality standards defined by the project.

One of the purposes of quality management is to find errors and defects as early in the project as possible. Therefore, a good quality management process will end up taking more effort hours and cost upfront. The goal is to reduce the chances that products or services will be of poor quality after the project has been completed.

Quality assurance is done not only to the products and services delivered by the project but also to the process and procedures used to manage the project, that includes the way the project uses the tools, techniques and methodologies to manage scope, schedule, budget and quality. Quality assurance also includes the project meets any legal or regulatory standards.

How will risks impact a project QUALITY?

Quality will be severely impacted because the project failed to produce the deliverables within scope, schedule, and budget.

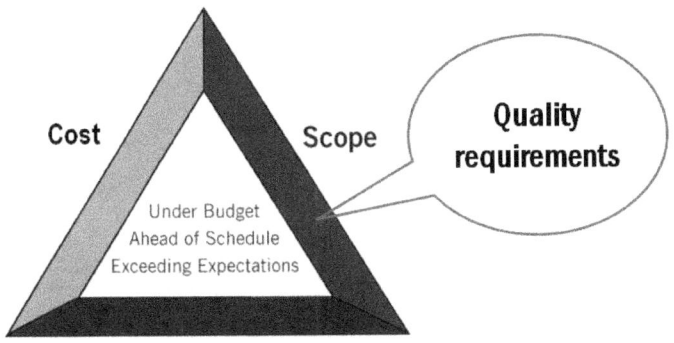

PROJECT BUDGET MUST INCLUDE A QA FUNCTION

The simple fact is that quality is an indispensable part of any effort (from both project management and system development perspectives). Building a product without quality controls is wrought with risk: it will not satisfy your customer, and will reflect poorly on your reputation. Assuming that you cannot do a change control to add a QA function to your Project Budget, the good news is that, in a pinch, you can do without a separate QA function by incorporating quality assurance into every procedure and task, and taking on quality control responsibilities yourself.

You need to incorporate rigorous review cycles into production and acceptance of every deliverable, by using peer review mechanisms as well as inviting external SME's. As is stated in the text above, "It is more important that the reviews be done than how they are done." Sometimes even having non-technical independent observers sitting in on reviews brings extra gravity and rigor to the proceedings. Another trick is getting the Customers even more closely involved in reviewing works in progress and providing feedback.

Finally, you will need to roll up your sleeves and personally check out test scripts and acceptance procedures, and join in the testing activities not necessarily to do any significant testing yourself, but to ensure that it gets done thoroughly and correctly.

WHO SHOULD BE DOING THE TESTING?

I can't trust the developers to check their own work! Can I? There are organizations where the testing function is separated into its own business unit. There are other organizations that have a separate QA function, but its members join the Project Teams at certain parts of the lifecycle, and perform testing on site. Finally, there are organizations that incorporate quality in everything they do, and thus have no separate QA function. Each approach has its own pluses and minuses, but the important concepts are:

1. Test plans and scripts need to be developed before any coding is done

2. Test scripts need to be executed faithfully, and the results communicated immediately to the developers
3. System development should not proceed until the defects have been corrected
4. The same defects in different testing cycles point to a serious problem that has to be resolved before any further work is done

CONTROL QUALITY

Quality control involves monitoring the project and its progress to determine if the quality assurance activities defined during Project Planning are being implemented and whether the results meet the quality standards defined during Project Initiation. The entire organization has responsibilities relating to quality, but the primary responsibility for ensuring that the project follows its defined quality procedures ultimately belongs to the Project Manager.

The purpose of quality management in projects is to ensure that the project outputs are delivered fit-for-purpose. If outputs are not fit-for-purpose, there is every likelihood that planned project outcomes will not be realized, or realized to a much lesser extent. It can be achieved by developing quality criteria for the outputs themselves and by ensuring that all project management processes are conducted in a quality manner. Quality management in a project increases certainty and reduces the risk of project failure. It involves a process for the management of changes, problems, issues and incidents that emerge during the production of the outputs. The management of this process may vary from project to project.

Conduct Peer Reviews – the goal of a peer review is to identify and remove quality issues from a deliverable as early and as efficiently as possible. A peer review is a thorough review of a specific deliverable, conducted by members of the Project Team who are the day-to-day peers of the individuals who produced the work.

Use Quality Checklists – both the Project Manager and Project Team members can create and make use of various checklists to be sure items are not overlooked while a product is being developed. Checklists may be simple hardcopy lists of "things to do," or may be generated using more formal, electronic-based tools. In either case, a checklist should be comprehensive and detailed enough to ensure that the resulting product or deliverable has been built to the level required to meet quality standards.

Maintain and Analyze the Project Schedule – this activity should never be taken lightly, regardless of the size of the project. Updating the Project Schedule on a regular basis while keeping a close watch on the timeline and budget is the primary mechanism to measure quality of the schedule.

Conduct Project Audits – the goal of a project audit is to ensure that the Quality Assurance activities defined in Project Planning are being implemented and to determine whether quality standards are being met. It is a process to note what is being done well, to identify real or potential issues, and to suggest ways for improvement.

QUALITY AUDITS

Quality audits are structured reviews of the quality management activities that help identify lessons learned that can improve the performance on current or future project activities. Audits are performed by project staff or consultants with expertise in specific areas. The purpose of quality audit is to review how the project is using its internal processes to produce the products and services it will deliver to the key project stakeholders. Its goal is to find ways to improve the tools, techniques and processes that create the products and services. If problems are detected during the quality audits, corrective action will be necessary to the tools, processes and procedures used to ensure quality is re-established. Part of the audit may include a review of the project staff understanding of the quality parameters or metrics, and skills expertise and knowledge of the people in charge of producing or delivering the products or services. If corrective actions are needed, these must be approved through the change control processes.

QUALITY MANAGEMENT VS QUALITY AUDIT

Quality Management is all the activities that are intended to bring about the desired level of quality. Quality Audit is the procedural control that ensure participants are adequately following the required procedures. These concepts are related, but should not be confused. In particular, Quality Audit relates to the approach to quality that is laid down in quality standards such as the ISO-900x standards.

THE PDCA CYCLE

The most popular tool used to determine quality assurance is the Shewhart Cycle. This cycle for quality assurance consists of four steps: Plan, Do, Check, and Act. These steps are commonly abbreviated as PDCA.

The four quality assurance steps within the PDCA model stand for:

- **Plan:** Establish objectives and processes required to deliver the desired results.

- **Do**: Implement the process developed.

- **Check**: Monitor and evaluate the implemented process by testing the results against the predetermined objectives

- **Act**: Apply actions necessary for improvement if the results require changes.

The PDCA is an effective method for monitoring quality assurance because it analyses existing conditions and methods used to provide the product or service to key project stakeholders. The goal is to ensure that excellence is inherent in every component of the process. Quality assurance also helps determine whether the steps used to provide the product or service are appropriate for the time and conditions. In addition, if the PDCA cycle is repeated throughout the lifetime of the project helping improve internal efficiency.

Quality assurance demands a degree of detail in order to be fully implemented at every step. Planning, for example, could include an investigation into the quality of the raw materials used in manufacturing, the actual assembly, or the inspection processes used. The Checking step could include beneficiary feedback or surveys to determine if beneficiary needs are being met or exceeded and why they are or are not. The acting could mean a total revision in the delivery process in order to correct a technical flaw. The goal to exceed stakeholder expectations in a measurable and accountable process is provided by quality assurance.

ASSURANCE VERSUS CONTROL

Quality assurance is often confused with quality control; quality control is done at the end of a process or activity to verify that quality standards have been met. Quality control by itself does not provide quality, although it may identify problems and suggest ways to improve it. In contrast, quality assurance is a systematic approach to obtaining quality standards. Quality assurance is something that must be planned for from the earliest stages of a project, with appropriate measures taken at every stage. Unfortunately, far too many development projects are implemented with no quality assurance plan, and these projects often fail to meet the quality expectations of the project sponsor and key project stakeholders. To avoid problems the project must be able to demonstrate consistent compliance with the quality requirements for the project.

Chapter 12 : QUALITY CONTROL

Quality control is the use of techniques and activities that compare actual quality performance with goals and define appropriate action in response to a shortfall. It is the process that monitors specific project results to determine if they comply with relevant standards and identifies different approaches to eliminate the causes for unsatisfactory performance. The goal of quality control is to improve quality and involves monitoring the project outputs to determine if they meet the quality standards or definitions based on the project stakeholder's expectations. Quality control also includes how the project performs in its efforts to manage scope, budget and schedule.

Quality Control focus on detection of defects

- A control mechanism installed to detect a failure before it occurs, serves as prevention.
- Eg. During process of cooking, alarm turns on to prevent overcooked food should the auto-cut off sensor malfunction and temperature goes beyond 80 degrees Celsius.

ACCEPTANCE

The key project stakeholders, the project sponsor or other key project stakeholders accept or reject the product or service delivered. Acceptance occurs after the key project stakeholders or project sponsor has had a chance to evaluate the product or service

Rework

Rework is the action taken to bring the rejected product or service into compliance with the requirements, quality specifications, or stakeholder expectations. Rework is expensive which is why the project must make every effort to do a good job in quality planning and quality assurance to avoid the need for rework. Rework and all the costs associated with it may not refundable by the project sponsor and the organization may end up covering those costs.

Adjustments

To correct or take the necessary steps to prevent further quality problems or defects based on quality control measurements. Adjustments are identified to the processes that produce the outputs and the decisions that were taken that lead to the defects and errors. Changes are taken to the Change Control processes of the project

Quality Control Tools

There are a couple of good tools that can be used to control the quality of the project, these are cause and effect diagrams, Pareto charts and control charts:

Cause and Effect Diagram

Also known as fishbone diagrams or Ishikawa diagrams (named after Kaoru Ishikawa, a Japanese quality control statistician, who developed the concept in the 1960s, and is considered one of the seven basic tools of quality management) It is named fishbone diagram because of their fish-like appearance, it is an analysis tool that provides a systematic way of looking at effects and the causes that create or contribute to those effects. The Ishikawa Diagram is employed by a problem-solving team as a tool for assembling all inputs (as to what are the causes of the problem they're addressing) systematically and graphically, with the inputs usually coming from a brainstorming session. It enables the team to focus on why the problem occurs, and not on the history or symptoms of the problem, or other topics that digress from the intent of the session. It also displays a real-time 'snapshot' of the collective inputs of the team as it is updated. The possible causes are presented at various levels of detail in connected branches, with the level of detail increasing as the branch goes outward, i.e., an outer branch is a cause of the inner branch it is attached to. Thus, the outermost branches usually indicate the root causes of the problem.

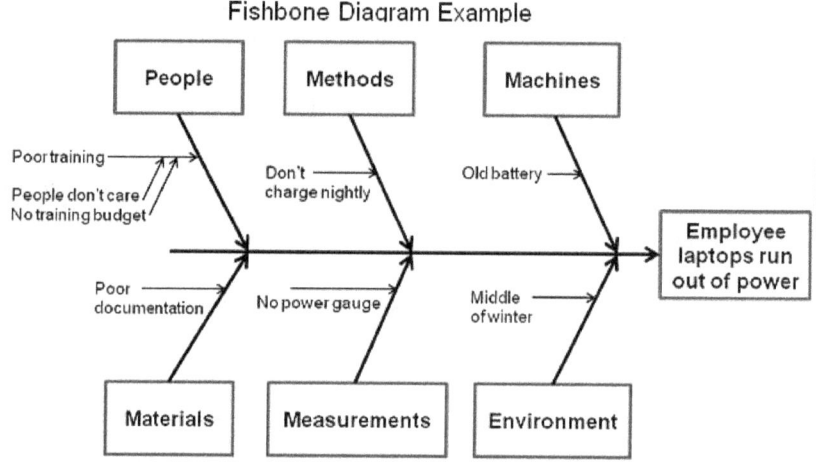

Fishbone Diagram Example

PARETO CHARTS

Based on Pareto's rule, which states that 80 percent of the problems are often due to 20 percent of the causes. The assumption is that most of the results in any situation are determined by a small number of causes and helps identify the vital few contributors that account for most quality problems.

The chart is a form of histogram that orders the data by frequency of occurrence; it shows how many defects were generated by a type of category of identified cause. For example, to determine the errors in the collection of beneficiary data the project team identified five causes and for each cause the frequency they contained errors, the data is plotted as shown in the chart above, the bars represent each category and the line the cumulative percentage of the errors, the chart allows to identify that 80% of the errors could be reduced just by improving the collection of data in two categories instead of focusing efforts to correct all categories.

CONTROL CHARTS

Control Chart is a graphical display of data that illustrates the results of a process over time, the purpose of a control chart is to prevent defects, rather than detect them or reject them, the chart allows the determine whether a process is in control or out of control over specified length of time. Control charts are often used to monitor the production of large quantities of products, but can also be used to monitor the volume and frequency of errors in documents, cost of schedule variances and other items related to project quality management. The figure below illustrates an example of a control chart for the process of controlling the weight of products manufactured by the key project stakeholders for sale in international markets. The customer has a limit tolerance for defects; these are the upper and lower control limits in the chart. Random examination of the products reveals data that once charted on the graph identifies the times when the production process created items that were outside the control limits, this helps the project determine actions to help the key project stakeholders improve the quality of their work.

Control charts can also be used in the project management areas, such as schedule and budget control, to determine whether the cost variances or schedule variances are outside the acceptable limits set by the project sponsor.

Quality Improvement

It is the systematic approach to the processes of work that looks to remove waste, loss, rework, frustration, etc. in order to make the processes of work more effective, efficient, and appropriate. Quality improvement refers to the application of methods and tools to close the gap between current and expected levels of quality by understanding and addressing system deficiencies and strengths to improve, or in some cases, re-design project processes.

A variety of quality improvement approaches exists, ranging from individual performance improvement to redesign of entire project processes. These approaches differ in terms of time, resources, and complexity, but share the same four steps in quality improvement:

- **Identify** what you want to improve; the project using the data found in the quality control process identifies the areas that need improvement.

- **Analyze** the problem or system, the team then investigates the causes for the problem and its implications to the project, the causes may be internal or external to the project.

- **Develop** potential solutions or changes that appear likely to improve the problem or system, the team brainstorms ideas and potential solutions to the problem, taking in consideration its impact to the project schedule and budget. After careful considerations the team decides and chooses the best alternative.

- **Test** and implement the solutions. The team may decide to test the solution on a small scale to verify that it is capable of fixing the problem, its testes for the initial assumptions made about the problem and once it confirms that the solution is a viable alternative, it then proceeds to implement in a full scale the solution.

Chapter 13 : COST OF QUALITY

The cost of quality is the sum of costs a project will spend to prevent poor quality and any other costs incurred as a result of outputs of poor quality. Poor quality is the waste, errors, or failure to meet stakeholder needs and project requirements. The costs of poor quality can be broken down into the three categories of prevention, appraisal, and failure costs:

PREVENTION COSTS

These are planned costs an organization incurs to ensure that errors are not made at any stage during the delivery process of that product or service to a beneficiary. Examples of prevention costs include:

- quality planning costs
- education and training costs
- quality administration staff costs
- process control costs
- market research costs
- field testing costs
- preventive maintenance costs.

The cost of preventing mistakes is always much less than the costs of inspection and correction.

APPRAISAL COSTS

These include the costs of verifying, checking, or evaluating a product or service during the delivery process. Examples of appraisal costs include receiving or incoming inspection costs, internal production audit costs, test and inspection costs, instrument maintenance costs, process measurement and control costs, supplier evaluation costs, and audit report costs.

Failure costs

A project incurs these costs because the product or service did not meet the requirements and had to be fixed or replaced, or the service had to be repeated.

Responsibilities for Quality

The Project Manager will, of course, have overall responsibility for the quality of the project. It is equally true that all participants have a role to play in delivering good results. Developing a quality culture amongst the team will normally generate greater value and satisfaction. Encourage the belief that the right level of quality is more important than getting things done fast. If there is a choice to be made between quality and progress it should be a matter for the Steering Committee to decide

Other managers will also be involved in the Quality Management process. In larger projects there may be a Quality Manager and Quality Team. Team Leaders and other senior staff will also be involved in the processes. In some environments, certain Quality Management functions may be performed by independent reviewers from outside the Project Team.

Change Control And Configuration Management

The purpose of Software Configuration Management is to establish and maintain the integrity of the products of the software project throughout the project's software life cycle. Software Configuration Management involves identifying configuration items for the software project, controlling these configuration items and changes to them, and recording and reporting status and change activity for these configuration items.

CONFIGURATION MANAGEMENT

Configuration Management (CM) refers to a discipline for evaluating, coordinating, approving or disapproving, and implementing changes in artifacts that are used to construct and maintain software systems. An artifact may be a piece of hardware or software or documentation. CM enables the management of artefacts from the initial concept through design, implementation, testing, baselining, building, release, and maintenance.

At its heart, CM is intended to eliminate the confusion and error brought about by the existence of different versions of artefacts. Artefact change is a fact of life: plan for it or plan to be overwhelmed by it. Changes are made to correct errors, provide enhancements, or simply reflect the evolutionary refinement of product definition. CM is about keeping the inevitable change under control. Without a well-enforced CM process, different team members (possibly at different sites) can use different versions of artefacts unintentionally; individuals can create versions without the proper authority; and the wrong version of an artefact can be used inadvertently.

Successful CM requires a well-defined and institutionalized set of policies and standards that clearly define

- the set of artefacts (configuration items) under the jurisdiction of CM
- how artefacts are named
- how artefacts enter and leave the controlled set
- how an artefact under CM is allowed to change
- What different versions of an artefact under CM are made available and under what conditions each one can be used
- how CM tools are used to enable and enforce CM

Software Configuration Management Process

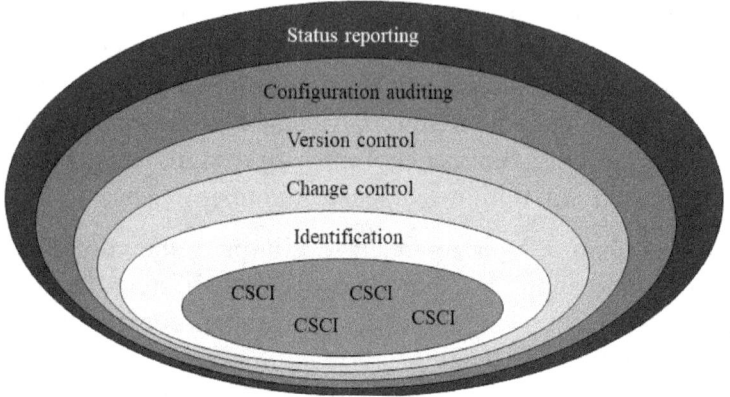

These policies and standards are documented in a CM plan that informs everyone in the organization just how CM is carried out.

Chapter 14 : SCOPE MANAGEMENT

It is important to remember that refinements to the Project Scope must include discussions and interviews with the Customer and other appropriate Stakeholders. The scope document, therefore, will reflect a mutual agreement between all parties, which is more likely to ensure that buy-in is achieved. A clearly defined Project Scope is critical to the success of a project. Without a clear definition work already performed may be subject to rework, resulting in lower team productivity in addition to increase in costs.

During System Initiation, a scope statement was written to document a basic description of the project and its deliverables. Refining the Project Scope breaks deliverables into smaller pieces of work, allowing the scope and the existing Project Budget, Schedule, and quality measurements to be more accurately defined. Where the initial Project Scope Statement highlighted the deliverables to be produced in support of the desired project output, the revised Project Scope must go one step further. Using the information learned during System Initiation, and based upon input gained by communicating regularly with the Customer and other appropriate Stakeholders, the Project Team must refine the Project Scope Statement to clearly verify each deliverable including an exact definition of what will be produced and what will not be produced.

Project Scope Management has several purposes:

- It defines what work is needed to complete the project objectives
- It determines what is included in the project
- It serves as a guide to determine what work is not needed to complete the project objectives
- It serves as a point of reference for what is not included in the project

A project scope is a description of the work required to deliver the product of a project.

The project scope defines what work will, and will not, be included in the project work. A project scope guides the project manager on decisions to add, change, or remove the work of the project. The project scope defines all of the required work, and only the required work, to complete the project.

Scope management is the process of ensuring that the project work is within scope and protecting the project from scope creep. The Project Scope Statement is the baseline for all future project decisions, as it justifies the business need of the project.

There are two types of scope:

- Product Scope - Defines the attributes of the product or service the project is creating
- Project Scope - Defines the required work of the project to create the product

PROJECT SCOPE VS. PRODUCT SCOPE

Project scope and product scope are different entities. A project scope deals with the required work to create the project deliverables. For instance, a project to create a new barn would focus only on the required work to complete the barn with the specific attributes, features, and characteristics called for by the Project Management plan. The scope of the project is specific to the work required to complete the project objectives.

A Product Scope is the attributes and characteristics of the deliverables the project is creating. As in the preceding barn project, the product scope would define the features and attributes of the barn. In this instance, the project to create a barn would not include creating a flower garden, a wading pool, and the installation of a fence. The product scope constitutes the characteristics and features of the product that the project creates.

The end result of the project is measured against the requirements for that product.

The Project Scope is the required work to deliver the product. Throughout the System Construction, the work is measured against the Project Management plan to verify that the project is on track to fulfil the product scope. The product scope is measured against requirements, while the project scope is measured against the Project Management plan

Changes to a Project Scope document must be made using a defined change control process. This process should include a description of the means by which scope will be managed and how changes to scope will be handled. Once documented, the process becomes part of the Project Management Plan. It is vital to document a clear description of how to determine when there is a change in scope to facilitate change control during System Construction and System Acceptance phase.

MANAGING SCOPE CHANGES

During System Design, the Project Manager, Project Sponsor, and Customer agreed on a formal change control process that was documented and included in the Project Management plan. The change control process describes:

- The definition of change and how to identify it
- How requests for change will be initiated
- How requests for change will be analyzed to determine if they are beneficial to the project
- The process to approve or reject change requests
- How funding will be secured to implement approved changes

Although changes can be expected to occur throughout every project phase, any negative effect on the project outcome should be avoidable if the change control process is executed and managed effectively.

Impact of Scope Creep

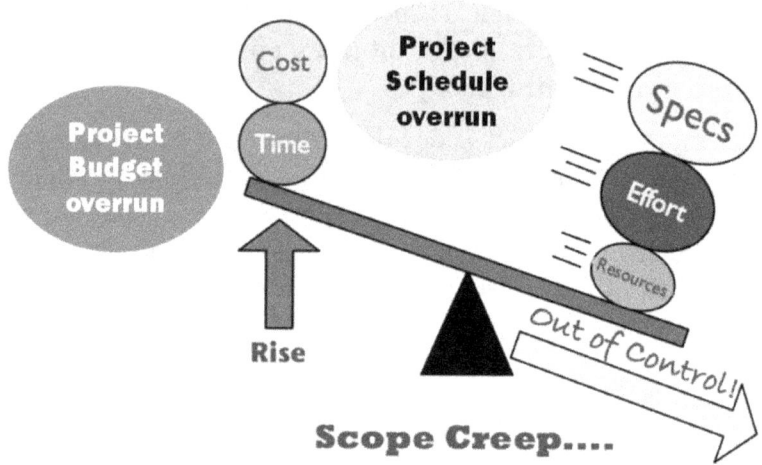

The need for change is usually discovered during System Construction, as actual task work is being performed. It is during System Construction that the Project Team may discover their original effort estimates were not accurate and will result in more or less effort being required to complete their work. It is also during System Construction that the Project Sponsor or Customer may realize that, despite their best efforts to thoroughly document the Project Scope, the product being produced is not exactly what they need. It is the responsibility of the Project Manager to keep a close watch on factors that could introduce potential "scope creep" and take proactive steps to prevent it from occurring, or to manage it as it occurs.

Sometimes change control is required if a Project Team member is not able to complete what was documented in the Project Scope, because of lack of skill, time constraints, or other factors outside his/her control. In most cases, these difficult to manage situations often result in lost time in the Project Schedule and can have a major impact on the project.

Sometimes change is simply informational and will most likely not affect the Project Scope or Schedule (e.g., the name of a Project Team member or the physical location of the Project Team offices may change). Changes that do not affect the project's cost, scope, schedule, and quality (CSSQ) do not need to follow the formal change control process, but should be documented in the Project Status Report or any other appropriate communication mechanism. However, for all changes that affect the project's CSSQ, it is vitally important for the Project Manager to implement and manage the change control process in every situation. Not doing so will cause confusion on the part of the Customer as to what constitutes a change. The change control process also helps maintain balance between the requirements of the project and the timeline and cost.

During System Design, individuals authorized to be requestors, reviewers, and approvers of change requests were identified and information about them was documented in the change control process. Change control begins when a requestor completes a change request form and submits it to the appropriate reviewers.

The role of the reviewers in the change control process is to analyze the request in terms of the level of effort and skill required to implement it. The reviewer, typically an expert in the subject area, will also make a recommendation to accept or reject the change request based upon its feasibility from a technical or implementation standpoint. He/she will communicate this information to the Project Manager and document it on the Change Request form. One of the roles of the Project Manager in the change control process is to analyze the reviewer's recommendation, and determine the overall effect of the requested change on the Project Schedule in terms of effort, cost, and resource requirements and availability. This information will be documented on the Change Request and presented to the approver.

The approver reviews the information and make a determination whether to approve the change request based upon the potential benefit of its implementation to the organization. If, for example, the implementation costs far outweigh the business benefit, the change request will most likely be rejected. A signature is required of all approvers, whether they are accepting or rejecting the request. If the request is being rejected, the approver must provide a reason. Once a change request has been approved, the Project Manager must incorporate the effect of the change into the Project Schedule. All affected tasks, estimated durations, dependencies, and resources must be modified. A new baseline should then be created for the amended schedule and budget. These become the new tools against which hours will be booked and project performance measured going forward.

CONTROL SCOPE

Control Scope is a process that concerned with ensuring that any changes to the project scope will be managed through the change control process, and to verify that the output from the project meets the requirements defined in the Project Scope.

SCOPE CREEP

Scope creep refers to increasing feature or additional functionality that is not included in the original Project Scope but the additional functionality is very important to the Customer, adding small yet time and resource-consuming features to the system once the scope of the project has been approved. For example, a project sponsor may try to add various bells and whistles to the project scope. Yet, scope creep does not always come from the project sponsor side. The project team itself may come across interesting or novel ideas as the project work progresses. Its enthusiasm for adding these ideas can divert its attention or add features and functions to the system that the project sponsor did not ask for and does not need. Scope creep must be identified and controlled throughout the project because it will lengthen the project schedule and, in turn, lead to cost overruns.

A scope change procedure should be in place before the actual work on the project commences. It can be part of, or at least referenced in, the Project Charter so that it is communicated to all project stakeholders. This procedure should allow for the identification and handling of all requested changes to the project's scope. Scope change requests can be made, and each request's impact on the project can be assessed. Then, a decision whether to accept or reject the scope change can be made.

Chapter 15 : LEADERSHIP MANAGEMENT

What Makes A Good Leader?

Although there are different styles of leadership, all effective leaders share certain characteristics. These are qualities that can be learned and improved upon over time.

Communication Skills

They communicate clearly. Managing a group, especially in the workplace, starts with good communication. Whether writing an e-mail or providing face-to-face employee feedback, good leaders say what they mean and mean what they say. They're not passive-aggressive, nor do they shy away from addressing challenges in a direct manner.

Passionate

They're passionate about their work. Many good leaders love what they do, and they're not afraid to show it. Of course, you can still be a good leader even if your professional and personal interests aren't a perfect match. Think about what you enjoy most in your work, and develop your enthusiasm around that you even may find that you're managing yourself into greater workplace satisfaction.

Unpopular

They don't care about being popular. In fact, if your first concern is whether everyone likes you, you may be less effective. Whether it's giving tough criticism or pointing out a practice you believe is unethical, learning how to be a good leader means getting comfortable doing or saying things that are best for your team and your organization, even if it makes you temporarily unpopular

Think Positive

They're positive and encouraging. Good leaders are uplifting. They praise employees for a job well done, taking time to coach and train if there are lapses in performance. In good times and bad, good leaders bring out the best in their employees by encouraging them to be their very best.

Connection

They build relationships. The ability to form productive connections is a key quality of a good leader. Strong managers aren't threatened by others. Instead of guarding their territory, they're constantly building bridges with others. A good leader knows the value of mutually beneficial relationships, and actively seeks them out.

Lead by Example

They lead by example. The best managers know that an essential part of what makes a good leader is setting the right example. From putting in extra hours on a major project to treating others with respect and kindness, good leaders show they're ready and willing to do anything they'd ask of their employees.

Innovation

Leaders must be able to do the job, but ability alone is not enough. True leadership requires a willingness to be bold, to consider unusual approaches to problems, to do more than just follow tried-and-true methods. Leaders are self-confident and have no need to put others down to feel good about themselves. They are willing to stand up for their ideas and debate them with others. This kind of intellectual competition is characteristic of a good leader.

Respect for Others

Balancing competition with respect may be difficult for young employees who think the way to get ahead is to outshine their coworkers. But neither workers nor supervisors like or respect leaders who think only of themselves. Above all, leadership requires the ability to get along with others in a variety of situations. For example, if you are class president, you won't be able to accomplish much if you begin to think too highly of yourself. Classmates you snub are not likely to volunteer to help with prom decorations. Likewise, if you are an assistant manager and ignore your coworkers until you need something, you will not always get the results you want.

Courteousness

Treat others as you would like to be treated. The workplace is still primarily a place where people interact. The social skills we have been practicing all our lives are important in business, too. In meetings, leaders must clearly communicate their ideas to team members, while still being open to suggestions from others. Corbis talking, avoiding sarcastic comments, and controlling emotional outbursts. Sarcasm and temper tantrums are not acceptable in a social setting and even less so in the workplace. Being in a supervisory position doesn't give you the right to be discourteous.

Sensitivity

Although they are important qualities, courtesy and agreeableness are not the only qualities of a good leader. He or she must also be sensitive to the feelings and needs of others. These needs are not always clearly expressed. Sometimes people do not even know what they want or need. Talented leaders are able to "read" the people around them and adjust their own behavior accordingly.

The aim of good management is to provide services to the community in an appropriate, efficient, equitable, and sustainable manner. This can only be achieved if key resources for service provision, including human resources, finances, hardware and process aspects of care delivery are brought together at the point of service delivery and are carefully synchronized. This chapter first discusses good management and leadership in general, then outlines relevant considerations for managing relations with patients and the district team, as well as finances and hardware and management schedules.

MANAGERS AND LEADERS

In the leadership development industry, there is a lot of confusion about the relationship between leadership and management. Many people use the terms interchangeably. Others see them as separate, but give different reasons why.

MANAGER	LEADER
• gives direction	• asks questions
• has subordinates	• has followers
• holds authority	• is motivational
• tells you what	• shows you how
• has good ideas	• actions good ideas
• reacts to change	• creates change
• tries to be a hero	• makes hereos
• exercises power	• develops power

Most dictionaries suggest leadership and management are quite similar in guiding or controlling a group of people to achieve a goal. Most web articles suggest that leadership and management are different, but offer contradictory reasons, such as: leadership inspires, management plans; leaders praise, managers find fault; leaders ask questions, managers give directions; etc. However, the qualities often ascribed to leadership can also apply to managers. There can be good and bad leaders, and there can be good and bad managers.

Management and leadership are important for the delivery of good health services. Although the two are similar in some respects, they may involve different types of outlooks, skills, and behaviors. Good managers should strive to be good leaders and good leaders, need management skills to be effective.

Leaders will have a vision of what can be achieved and then communicate this to others and evolve strategies for realizing the vision. They motivate people and are able to negotiate for resources and other support to achieve their goals.

Managers ensure that the available resources are well organized and applied to produce the best results. In the resource-constrained and difficult environments of many low to middle-income countries, a manager must also be a leader to achieve optimum results.

WHAT ARE THE ATTRIBUTES OF A GOOD LEADER?

Leaders often (but not necessarily always):

- have a sense of mission;
- are charismatic;
- are able to influence people to work together for a common cause;
- are decisive;
- use creative problem solving to promote better care and a positive working environment

LEADERSHIP AND MANAGEMENT

There is an essential difference between leadership and management which is captured in these definitions:

- Leadership is setting a new direction or vision for a group that they follow, i.e.: a leader is the spearhead for that new direction.
- Management controls or directs people/resources in a group according to principles or values that have been established.

There is much more to these definitions than may at first appear. Albert Einstein said that everything should be made as simple as possible but no simpler. However, it is an oversimplification to think that leaders lead and followers follow, because the relationship between leadership, management, and followers is a complex one. Also, leadership and management are often part of the same role because there is a continual adjustment of the direction (leadership) and controlling resources to achieve that direction (management). We can see the difference more clearly by looking at some examples of leadership without management, and management without leadership.

LEADERSHIP WITHOUT MANAGEMENT

The difference between leadership and management can be illustrated by considering instances when there is one without the other. Leadership without management sets a direction or vision that others follow, without considering how the new direction is going to be achieved. Other people then have to work hard in the trail that is left behind, picking up the pieces and making it work.

You can see an example of this in Lord of the Rings. At the council of Elrond, there is an argument about how they should proceed. Frodo Baggins rescues the council from the conflict by taking responsibility for destroying the ring. He sets a direction but has no idea how to go about it. During the quest, most of the management of the group comes from others, particularly Gandalf and Aragorn.

There can be leaders who don't manage in the workplace. For example, an entrepreneur might grow a business by networking, building relationships, and generating ideas for new products. However, he/she might also rely on a deputy e.g., a factory manager to ensure the right staff are recruited, products or services are produced, and the business is delivered.

MANAGEMENT WITHOUT LEADERSHIP

Management without leadership controls resources to maintain the status quo or ensure things happen according to already-established plans. For example, a sports referee manages opposing teams to ensure they keep within the rules of the game. However, a referee does not usually provide "leadership" because there is no new change, no new direction. Also, what is often referred to as "participative management" can be a very effective form of leadership. In this approach, a new direction may seem to emerge from the group rather than the leader. However, the leader has facilitated that new direction whilst also engendering ownership within the group i.e., it is an advanced form of leadership.

SYMBOLIC LEADERSHIP

Sometimes, an individual may act as a figurehead for change and be viewed as a leader even though he/she hasn't set any new direction. This can arise when a group sets a direction of its own accord, and needs a spearhead in order to express it.

In prison, Nelson Mandela was an example of symbolic leadership. Although his ability to take action was limited, he continued to grow in power and influence (as the symbolic leader for the anti-apartheid movement). This power came from the mass movement, from the group that are nominally viewed as the followers. Following his release from prison, he demonstrated actual leadership by leading South Africa into a process of reconciliation rather than retribution. This illustrates the complexity of the relationship between leaders, followers, and context. A leader's power often comes from the followers. For example, in democratic government, leaders are elected because of the direction they offer e.g., for economic growth or social development. However, if they subsequently pursue a direction that is different from the expectations of the electorate, they may lose the next election, or even provoke civil unrest beforehand.

LEADERSHIP STYLES

There are many different types of leadership (or management) style. Different situations, groups, or cultures, may require the use of different styles in order to set a direction or ensure that it is followed.

BEING INNOVATIVE

As leadership involves setting a new visionary direction e.g., JFK setting the goal of putting a man on the moon. As management involves producing creative ideas to ensure the vision is realized e.g., coming up with ideas that enabled Apollo 13 to return safely to earth.

PARTICIPATIVE MANAGEMENT

As leadership involves facilitating a new direction through team discussion. As management involves winning the commitment of a team to a defined goal. Everyone has their own preferred set of leadership styles. One aspect of becoming an effective is to build greater awareness of those styles, learning how to harness them productively, and mitigating natural weaknesses.

ORGANIZATIONAL GOVERNANCE

The key ingredients to project management are people, processes, and technology. Technology is a tool, while processes provide a structure and path for managing and carrying out the project. The success of a project, however, is often determined by the various project stakeholders, as well as who is (or who is not) on the project team. In this chapter, we will discuss the human resources of project management. The area of project human resource management entails:

- organizational planning
- staff acquisition
- team development.

Project Organization

Key project management committees that are responsible for project delivery and implementation

ORGANIZATION PLANNING

Organization planning focuses on the roles, responsibilities, and relationships among the project stakeholders. These individuals or groups can be internal or external to the project. Moreover, organizational planning involves creating a project structure that will support the project processes and stakeholders so that the project is carried out efficiently and effectively.

STAFF ACQUISITION

Staff acquisition includes staffing the project with the best available human resources. Effective staffing involves having policies, procedures, and practices to guide the recruitment of appropriately skilled and experienced staff. Moreover, it may include negotiating for staff from other functional areas within the organization.

TEAM DEVELOPMENT

Team development involves creating an environment to develop and support the individual team members and the team itself.

This chapter will expand upon these three subjects and integrate several relatively recent concepts for understanding the governance structure in project management. Three primary organizational structure: the functional, project, and matrix will be described. In addition, the various opportunities and challenges for projects conducted under each structure will be discussed. As an Engineering Manager or project team member, it is important to understand an organization's structure since this will determine authorities, roles, responsibilities, communication channels, and availability of resources.

Nothing can be achieved without team effort

In Project Management, the project team carries out the work needed to complete the project.

Once the project team is in place, it is important that the project team learn from each other and from past project experiences. Thus, the idea of learning cycles will be introduced as a tool for team learning and for capturing lessons learned that can be documented, stored, and retrieved using a knowledge management system

PROJECT STAKEHOLDERS

Stakeholders are individuals, groups, or even organizations that have a stake, or claim, in the project's outcome. Often, we think of stakeholders as only those individuals or groups having an interest in the successful outcome of a project, but the sad truth is that there are many who can gain from a project's failure. While the formal organization tells us a little about the stakeholders and what their interests may be, the informal organization paints a much more interesting picture.

BUDGET MANAGEMENT

Engineering Manager must be capable to prepare the project budget. All businesses have a responsibility to the monies they are allotted, have earned, and have acquired through donations. In project management, the work completed within a project must be measured for value and accounted for. The budget the organization has set for the project must be guarded. Ultimately, the success of the project should generate an increase in funds, productivity, or efficiency for the sponsoring organization.

PROJECT RESOURCES

Engineering Manager must be organized. How much time has been wasted looking for documentation, contracts, or permits? How much money has been lost due to disorganization? How many projects have failed because the Engineering Manager did not keep and maintain accurate records? Organization is a methodical approach to storing and retrieving information, as it is needed. Organization does not require a spotless desk, thousands of labeled file folders, or archives of every project-related document. Organization requires thorough, fast, and reliable access to project data.

TEAM LEADERSHIP

Managing a project team is different from leading a project team. It has been said that you manage things, but lead people. In project management, you must create a relationship between the project team members and yourself to excite, motivate, and inspire the workers to move toward the strategy and vision of the project deliverable.

People Management

People management requires several soft skills, including those that can lead to open and honest communication as well as improved employee experience. Each of these skills can better help you interact with your employees and perform organizational tasks.

Here are eight essential people management skills to incorporate into your workplace:

1. Empowering employees
2. Active listening
3. Conflict-resolution
4. Flexibility
5. Patience
6. Clear communication
7. Trust
8. Organization

Empowering Employees

Empowering your employees helps them develop new skills and be more productive. It's important to train new employees well and give them the knowledge and resources they need to perform assigned tasks and continue learning on their own.

Other important aspects of empowering employees include:

- Offering constructive feedback to encourage skill-building
- Being available for questions or additional training

- Allowing them to adjust workflow or standard processes if it improves their productivity
- Encouraging them to take additional skill-building courses and learning opportunities
- Supporting them on or managing challenging projects

ACTIVE LISTENING

Active listening is the practice of listening to the speaker to fully understand their perspective, question or concern before responding. Active listeners remove distractions, maintain eye contact and offer verbal or non-verbal cues to indicate their engagement and understanding. When an employee comes to you with a question or issue, use nonverbal cues such as nodding to demonstrate your engagement while they're speaking. Respond thoughtfully by repeating a summary of your understanding of their message.

If you have understood, you can then ask follow-up questions to learn more about what they need. You can also express that you empathize with their experience to further assure them you understand and respect them. These active listening techniques lead to quality people management that promotes positive interactions in the workplace.

CONFLICT-RESOLUTION

Good conflict-resolution skills can help address interpersonal challenges. You can analyze the situation and identify what the causes of the conflict might be. If there's a miscommunication or differing opinions, you can mediate between opposing parties and help them make a compromise or reach a collective understanding. After mediation, monitor the situation to ensure the conflict is fully resolved and to prevent it from occurring again.

FLEXIBILITY

Knowing when to be flexible and when to more firmly direct employees is an important aspect of effective people management. You can demonstrate flexibility in your management style by accommodating individual employee needs such as adjustable schedules or remote work options—and allowing employees to adjust their individual workflow so they can be as productive as possible. You should assess the results of the employee's process to ensure its efficiency and to help them revise the process if it can be optimized. For example, if one of your employees prefers to complete related tasks in batches while another employee moves back and forth between different tasks, analyze each employee's results. If both employees are their most productive using their respective processes, then you can encourage them to continue using and improving their systems. You may even ask them to demonstrate their individual processes to other employees to optimize the entire team's workflow. If an employee seems to be struggling with personalizing their process, you can coach them through the standard steps, and help them discover what works best for them.

PATIENCE

Patience is an important people management skill that uses kindness, respect and empathy while helping others overcome obstacles. You can use patience when training new employees, teaching new processes, handling conflicts or solving problems. When employees can trust their managers to be patient, they are more likely to ask for clarification to ensure they understand directions and to increase the quality of their work. For example, if an employee continues asking questions about a single process, you should continue to guide them while trying new ways to better communicate your message. Consider providing multiple examples that clarify and demonstrate your instructions, or combine typed instructions with visual diagrams if possible.

CLEAR COMMUNICATION

Communication is a necessary people management skill that enables team members to work together in solving problems, brainstorming new ideas and adapting to new changes. Your ability to clearly communicate with your coworkers can help you be a better team member. Practice effective communication by using clear and simple language so every recipient understands your message. Consider revising the way you give your message to avoid common barriers, such as too much information at one time or inaccessible terms. Allow your employees to ask clarifying questions, and directly confirm that each member of your team understands the information so there is no miscommunication.

TRUST

Trust means believing that you can rely on someone's abilities, assistance or advice when you need it most. Building trust helps your team work together more efficiently and productively. Teams should be able to trust that their leader supports them and believes in their hard work. Leaders should be able to trust that their team can complete tasks correctly and on time. You can build trust by reliably performing your tasks and demonstrating technical skills when employees ask for help. You can also promote trust when you provide constructive feedback that helps team members improve their skills and work quality.

ORGANIZATION

Managing a team involves handling several different ongoing tasks simultaneously. Being organized is an important people management skill that helps you track and maintain your team's productivity.

Signs of effective organization include:

- Promptly responding to emails, approval requests and questions
- Keeping a calendar to actively track deadlines
- Running meetings that efficiently discuss information
- Properly assigning tasks to team members
- See your instant resume report
- Get recommendations for your resume in minutes

Chapter 16 : TEAM COLLABORATION

Team collaboration is the healthcare facilities management officer's ability to lead a group of people in accomplishing a task or common goal. Effective team collaboration involves supporting, communicating with and uplifting team members so they perform to the best of their abilities and continue to grow as professionals. Precisely what constitutes effective team collaboration, however, may differ depending on the work environment and the people. Some managers do well with an authoritative approach, while other managers prefer to manage their teams in a more casual way. Some team members may also respond differently to certain management styles. Understanding your own leadership style and what works best with your team is an important part of team collaboration.

WHY IS TEAM COLLABORATION IMPORTANT IN FACILITIES MANAGEMENT?

Team collaboration is important for a number of reasons within the workplace:

- It promotes a unified approach to leadership within a company or team, especially when team building is implemented.
- It makes it easier to solve problems through the implementation of negotiating and critical thinking.
- It encourages open communication between managers and team members and emphasizes good communication skills and active listening.
- It ensures managers and team members are working toward a common goal that has been clearly defined.

It helps managers clearly outline the roles and expectations for their team members. Understanding the importance of team collaboration and working to develop your team management skills can help you be the most effective leader possible. The more effective you're at managing your team, the more successful your team will be within the workplace.

What Are The Benefits of Team Collaboration?

* Increases productivity
* Improves decision-making
* Increases creativity and innovation
* Enhances problem-solving skills
* Greater job satisfaction

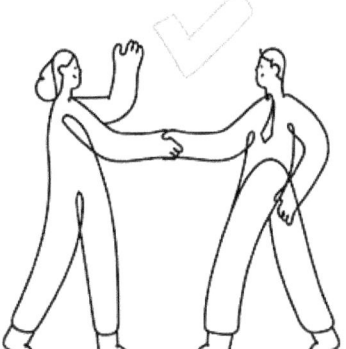

EXAMPLES OF EFFECTIVE TEAM COLLABORATION SKILLS

Effective team managers tend to share certain skills, attitudes and tactics. Although good management involves more than merely applying a list of tried-and-tested methods and approaches, you may benefit from considering practices that have worked well for other managers over the years. If you're new in management or wish to grow your management skills, here are a few ways you can hone your skills as a team leader as well as real-life examples within the workplace.

FOCUS ON SERVING RATHER THAN MANAGING

Although it may seem counter-intuitive, effective managers focus on serving rather than managing their teams. As a manager, you should at all times have the best interests of your team members in mind and should strive to assist and support them in achieving both individual and team goals. In addition, a good manager leads through actions, as opposed to merely giving orders and delegating tasks. If you want your team to act professionally and deliver excellent work, you should act accordingly and set an example.

Example: A team member has phoned to say she is ill and not coming into work. Instead of adding all of her outstanding tasks to the workload of other team members, you offer to complete some of the tasks yourself.

DON'T ALWAYS ASSUME YOU'RE RIGHT

If you want to be a good manager, you have to be open to continuously learning. While as a manager you may occupy a more senior position than the team members you manage, you should keep an open mind as to what your employees can teach you on a daily basis. Apart from learning from your team, you should also ensure that you stay up-to-date with the latest trends and developments and invest in your own ongoing professional development.

Example: During a meeting with your team, you give your opinion about a technical issue that one of your clients is experiencing. One of your senior technicians responds to your analysis with a different point of view. Instead of immediately assuming your viewpoint is correct, you listen attentively to what he has to say and then have a constructive discussion on the matter.

MAKE TRANSPARENCY A PRIORITY

A transparent workplace can help employees feel more connected and encourage creativity and accountability. Practicing transparency through open and consistent communication allows your team members to feel a sense of respect which is important for overall job satisfaction and productivity. This can also help your team members have more confidence when it comes to contributing ideas and solutions to the workplace, which can ultimately benefit everyone involved.

Example: Rather than distributing team tasks on an individual basis, use a project management system to assign and display tasks and overall goals for a particular project. When team members can clearly see their roles in a project and know exactly what their responsibilities are, they are more likely to hold themselves accountable for producing quality work.

SET BOUNDARIES

Although you want to treat your team with kindness and respect, it is also important to set boundaries and assert your authority at times. Team members should know that your job is to ensure their work gets done efficiently and that, when necessary, you will take disciplinary action. There should be a very clear understanding of responsibilities and roles within the workspace to discourage team members from challenging unclear boundaries.

Example: A client has informed you that one of your technicians has not been attending to the necessary maintenance tasks on a regular basis as per their service agreement. Rather than sending an email to let your technician know they need to update the maintenance tasks, you meet with them in person to clearly outline your expectations and discuss the employee's recent unsatisfactory performance. By meeting in person, you show your team member that you take their performance seriously and that not following through on work assignments will not be tolerated.

Provide a Positive Workspace

Although the business world is a serious place that often involves profit margins, risk assessments and performance evaluations, studies have shown that a bit of humor and light-heartedness in the office can have a remarkably positive effect on productivity. If possible, organize fun work outings or liven up the office environment with some plants and bright colors. Even if you just bring a bunch of flowers to work or tell a joke every now and then, this can brighten your team's day and foster a culture of happiness within the workspace.

Example: The morale in the office is a bit low after losing a big account. You decide to lighten up the mood by hiring a mobile massage therapist to give everyone a shoulder and neck massage. When everyone is a bit more relaxed you sit them down with doughnuts and coffee to discuss lessons learned and how the team can improve on service delivery in the future.

Emphasize Constant and Effective Communication Within the Workplace

One of the most important aspects of effective management is communication. As a manager, you should provide your team with all the relevant information at all times as well as encourage feedback from your employees. As effective communication starts with attentive listening, you should set an example to your team members by really listening to them and considering their opinions and input. You should also strive to foster a work environment where team members have the freedom to express themselves in a polite and respectful manner. Constructive and positive communication does, however, not always involve talking in person. There is an array of social media apps available today through which co-workers can stay in touch with each other and exchange ideas.

Example: You realize there is a lack of communication in the office, which is negatively affecting service delivery. To address this issue, you call a meeting with team members where you discuss processes and where the breakdown in communication is taking place. To assist team members, you provide them with a mobile application on their phones where they can input the necessary updates when they are working outside of the office space.

ENCOURAGE AND NURTURE YOUR TEAM'S GROWTH

As a manager, you should support and nurture your team. Your staff should know you have their personal development and best interests at heart and that you're supportive of their goals and dreams. This means that you should always be on the lookout for ways to develop and enrich your team, such as providing them with opportunities to attend workshops and conferences and stay up-to-date through training and certification. Apart from encouraging your workers to continuously expand their knowledge, you can also nurture and motivate them through positive feedback for good work or improvement in performance. However, you should also provide constructive criticism at times, as this can assist team members in their professional development.

Example: An exciting conference is taking place which involves new technology. Although only senior engineers and management typically attend conferences, you have a talented junior engineer in your team who can benefit from going to the conference. You decide to raise this matter in the next management meeting and request that they allow the junior engineer to attend.

BE OPEN TO CHANGE

To be an effective manager you need to be open to change. This involves adapting your management style when necessary and realizing that different team members may have different approaches and ways of doing things. Be open to trying new technologies and to changing your typical method of management when it no longer produces the desired outcomes.

POSITIVE WAYS TO LEAD BY EXAMPLE IN THE WORKPLACE

A workplace can benefit from having influential leaders in place to guide employees. As a leader, your team looks to you for inspiration, encouragement and direction. You can provide this by leading by example and building a culture of trust and accountability. Leading by example means guiding others through your behaviors and inspiring them to do the same as you. It is a leadership style servant leadership where you model the behavior you want to see in your team.

When you lead by example, you provide a path to direct others so that everyone works toward a goal with the same purpose. A leader makes it natural for people to feel like they want to do the best for the organization they work for. Leading by example can accomplish this and create a workplace filled with trust, confidence and purpose.

BENEFITS OF LEADING BY EXAMPLE IN THE WORKPLACE

Many benefits come from leading by example whether you're an executive or a junior associate. The benefits of having someone or multiple people in the workplace who led by example include:

More respect and trust

Someone who leads by example can expect to receive respect from their superiors, people who work alongside them and their employees. They are able to:

- Inspire confidence in others
- Understand the workplace and how everyone works together
- Stick to their word and actively seek solutions to problems
- Form a workplace culture that celebrates everyone's skill set
- Involve every member of the team in projects or important decisions

Higher productivity

When you lead by example, your team will soon follow, working just as hard and accomplishing just as much as you to do their part for the organization. They will strive to make their team proud and not let anyone down by performing below their abilities.

Loyal employees

Leading by example inspires those around you to enjoy being part of the team and a company employee. They want to enjoy the people they work with, including their leader. Satisfied employees have lower absenteeism, are more positive, contribute more to discussions, volunteer to take on more projects or help a coworker.

COMMITMENT TO THE ORGANIZATION

When there is positive leadership, employees are generally more committed to the company. They strive to help achieve its goals, develop a team mentality and work to support the company's mission, purpose and values. When a leader leads by example and works alongside their team, they inspire others to do the same.

BENCHMARK STANDARDS

A leader's actions set the standard for behavior in the workplace. How you act can determine how team members respond. For example, if you're always on time for meetings, your team will be more likely to do the same. On the other hand, if you don't communicate with your employees, you may notice the workplace becomes siloed and non-collaborative.

Chapter 17 : COMMUNICATION SKILLS

Communication Skills is the most important skills across any profession

ELECTRONIC COMMUNICATION

There are many forms of electronic communication today, you can communicate via X (formerly known as Twitter), WhatsApp, e-mail, Skype, short messaging service, Telegram, and many other chat applications.

Electronic communication places new demands on language that leads to interesting variations in written language use. Hailed as a powerful educational resource, the electronic communication medium has not only revolutionized the composing process but has also been found to encourage participation in writing activity.

One reason for this is that e-mail and online chats provide a non-threatening atmosphere in which writers feel less inhibited about expressing themselves, encouraging even timid students who usually refuse to speak in face-to-face discussions to actively participate in online chats. Another reason is that the Web provides an arena for writers to present their work to a real and larger audience that extends beyond classroom and school boundaries. When students realize that they are going to put their work on the Web for readers in the real world, they are motivated to write. The electronic communication medium has been found to increase collaborative writing activities. There are mixed views on whether it has a similar effect on the quantity and quality of writing done by individual students.

Because the electronic communication medium reduces the intimidation factor and offers attractive features, it improves students' attitudes towards writing and practicing the target language and encourages students to produce more text. The quality of all relationships is formed and maintained much more through non-verbal communication than through words, which play a relatively minor part. Becoming skilled in reading and interpreting non-verbal behavior is essential to enhancing effectiveness in all relationships and in helping patients. Learning about our own non-verbal behavior, and using that knowledge to influence how we relate to others will help us to see below the surface and to be more useful and successful in everything we do. Physical, and non-verbal elements of the environment also contribute significantly to the messages that patients receive and to their reactions to healthcare. Blindness to non-verbal behavior is almost complete blindness to the meaning and complexity of all communication, of who other people really are and what they are communicating or trying to conceal.

Communication skills are abilities you use when giving and receiving different kinds of information. While these skills may be a regular part of your day-to-day work life, communicating in a clear, effective and efficient way is an extremely special and useful skill. Learning from great communicators around you and actively practicing ways to improve your communications over time will certainly support your efforts to achieve various personal and professional goals. Communication skills involve listening, speaking, observing and empathizing. It is also helpful to understand the differences in how to communicate through face-to-face interactions, phone conversations and digital communications, like email and social media.

There are four main types of communication you might use on a daily basis, including:

- Verbal: Communicating by way of a spoken language.

- Nonverbal: Communicating by way of body language, facial expressions and vocalics.

- Written: Communicating by way of written language, symbols and numbers.

- Visual: Communication by way of photography, art, drawings, sketches, charts and graphs.

E-MAIL COMMUNICATION

Electronic Mail or e-mail is a system of electronic correspondence by which users send and receive messages over a network of computer and telecommunication links. The message may consist of short notes and greetings, or extensive text files plus graphics and photographic images, video clips or sound. Thus, e-mail is an 'electronic past office'. It lets people communicate even in the absence of the receiver at the other end. It means that you can send e-mail message at any time or whenever you want. The person, to whom you have sent the message, can read the same whenever he wants. Thus, the sender and the receiver don't have to connect themselves at the same time to communicate that particular message.

ADVANTAGES OF E-MAIL

- It permits sending to and receiving messages from others having e-mail address.
- It transmits the message almost immediately. Thus, its speed is very fast.
- It does not require the presence of the receiver of the message at the other end. The message is delivered into his mailbox and it can be checked by the receiver by opening his mailbox at any time.
- It directly reaches the concerned individual's electronic mailbox.
- It ensures a higher degree of secrecy of the message.

- It is a very cheap medium of communication. Hard copy letters and memorandums can often be replaced by electronic mail.
- Message can be sent at any time, day or night, eliminating problems brought about by differences in time zone.
- Identical messages can be sent to many people simultaneously.

E-MAIL ETIQUETTES

- Respond to an e-mail within 24 hours.
- For convenience of receiver, provide clearly worded subject lines for all messages.
- Use short paragraph for gaining reader's attention.
- Be complete and concise.
- Use upper and lower-case letters for clarity purposes.
- Inappropriate and unpleasant words must be avoided.
- Avoid adding many attachments to your message.
- Always apply personal name if your mail system allows it.
- Re-read and proof read the message before sending.
- Use grammar checker before sending.

If you have access to your boss's e-mail account, I would suggest you regularly read the e-mails, even if they deal with them themselves. It is always useful to be well informed and to have a broad picture of what they are doing.

Remember to put a heading in the subject in your e-mail. Everyone gets so much e-mail and may scan their in-box for ones they feel they need to read urgently, so make the heading something that will entice them to open it and read it. They may use also the subject heading to file their e-mails by. It is important to remember that if you pick up an e-mail to reply to it, you need to change the subject heading if you are emailing about a different subject. E-mails are easy to send but so difficult to retrieve (if at all), and when writing them you should carefully consider the tone and message conveyed. They must be professional, with correct grammar and spelling. You must also make sure they are sent to the correct recipients, with everyone copied in who should be. It is important not to type in capital letters as this is considered to be shouting on e-mail. Also, the human eye finds it easier to read small letters than capitals. If you want to do headings you can make them bold.

Be careful when sending group e-mails that you do not give away people's e-mail addresses against their wishes. You should use blind copy (bcc) to keep the e-mail addresses of each recipient private. Be careful of how you word e-mails and how they read think about how it will come across to the recipient. If you are angry about something don't send off an e-mail in haste: think about it, draft it and go back to it later when you have calmed down; change it or delete it if necessary, and remember it is sometimes better to pick up a phone or meet face to face.

E-mails that are quite curt, short and to the point are sometimes perceived as coming from someone who is abrupt or arrogant. They can irritate some people even though you may be doing it this way because of lack of time. You should write an e-mail, then read it from the reader's point of view imagining how the wording could be interpreted. Messages should always have a greeting at the beginning and be signed off at the end. It is a good idea to use 'signatures', which may include a farewell greeting such as 'kind regards and your full contact details to help the recipients should they want to call you. Similarly, people do not want to receive long e-mails that ramble on but rather ones that are to the point. If it is necessary to give lots of information, this should be attached as a word document rather than in the e-mail itself. Be very careful with sending confidential information in emails as they can be forwarded on and can be read by the company if the authorities so wish. Consider whether it would be better to post or deliver highly confidential material by hand.

Also be aware of your company's e-mail etiquette. Use your personal e-mail address for personal e-mails rather than clogging up the company's inbox with your personal correspondence. Be careful not to use work time for your personal concerns.

COMMUNICATING EFFECTIVELY IN THE WORKPLACE

While there are several communication skills you will use in different scenarios, there are a few ways you can be an effective communicator at work.

Clear and Concise

Making your message as easy to consume as possible reduces the chance of misunderstandings, speeds up projects and helps others quickly understand your goals. Instead of speaking in long, detailed sentences, practice reducing your message down to its core meaning. While providing context is helpful, it is best to give the most necessary information when trying to communicate your idea, instruction or message.

Empathy

Understanding your colleague's feelings, ideas and goals can help you when communicating with them. For example, you might need help from other departments to get a project started. If they are not willing to help or have concerns, practicing empathy can help you position your message in a way that addresses their apprehension.

Assertive

At times, it is necessary to be assertive to reach your goals whether you are asking for a raise, seeking project opportunities or resisting an idea you don't think will be beneficial. While presenting with confidence is an important part of the workplace, you should always be respectful in conversation. Keeping an even tone and providing sound reasons for your assertions will help others be receptive to your thoughts.

Calm and Consistent

When there is a disagreement or conflict, it can be easy to bring emotion into your communications. It is important to remain calm when communicating with others in the workplace. Be aware of your body language by not crossing your arms or rolling your eyes. Maintaining consistent body language and keeping an even tone of voice can help you reach a conclusion peacefully and productively.

ANSWERING THE PHONE

Answer the phone with a smile on your face. The smile can be 'heard' and you will sound happy and pleasant. If you are extremely busy and getting stressed with your work, take a deep breath before you answer the phone to calm you down and make you sound normal and not anxious. Answer the phone promptly don't let it ring more than three times before you answer it. Set yourself a daily challenge to attempt to answer the phone on the first ring so that callers are not kept holding on the line for longer than is necessary, they will appreciate not having their time wasted. This helps exceed expectations when you are consistent. Always be polite, helpful and proactive when dealing with phone calls. Whenever you can, go that extra mile to help the caller or client it always pays off and sometimes it gets back to your boss how helpful you have been. It improves the perception of the company and client relationships as well as your own reputation and relationships.

Always try to help the callers when they ask for your boss. You will often be quite capable of dealing with the call yourself and it is amazing how many times all the caller wants is some information that you can provide. Find out as much information as possible and if appropriate make notes of the call, then inform your boss as soon as possible and get back to the caller. Callers do not always realize that you can do a lot more than just an answering machine so you have to ask probing questions.

COMMUNICATING WITH DIFFERENT CULTURES

Often, we can see the reason behind our own cultural ways and habits, but others may not see them in the same way. The habits, words and gestures of people from different cultures may seem odd and confusing to us. We are increasingly working across cultures and we should be aware and respectful of each other's norms and differing etiquette. If your boss visits another country, research any cultural differences for that country to make sure the boss does not offend anyone. The ritual of shaking hands is especially important and, particularly for women, the dress code. It is a good idea to provide translations of some basic greeting words 'hello, how are you', 'thank you', 'goodbye' and so on. If possible, when planning to do business in other countries it is advisable to try to spend a day or two there beforehand to do some 'on the ground' research. If time affords then suggest this to your boss and schedule it in the diary. Some countries take a much more direct and focused approach than others, while some will require 'small talk' and relationship building before doing business.

Working with different cultures means that there will be a need for clarity in the communications we make and we should watch and listen and learn from others. However, it is worth remembering that respect, openness and courtesy are common to all cultures. Never assume that others think the same. Even people in the same culture may be brought up in a different environment, which makes them differ from each other. Observe people before you do or say anything that may cause misunderstanding or offend another person. Be careful with the English language as it can cause confusion. The meanings of words and phrases may vary in different English-speaking countries such as the UK, Australia, South Africa and the United States.

Body language also means different things in different countries. The common English and American 'thumbs up' (well done) gesture, for example, would be offensive in some countries. Making eye contact, showing the sole of your foot, personal space, sitting down before the other person, reading a business card, and presenting an object with your left hand all these gestures and behaviors can convey very different impressions. Be warned and watch and listen and learn.

Written Communication

Written communication is best suited when the communicator and the receiver are beyond the oral communication medium. The executives in all organizations can maintain effective inter-departmental and intra-departmental connections through messages in written words. The process of communication involves sending a message in written words. Written communication covers all kinds of subject matter like notices, memorandums, reports, financial statements, business letters, etc. This type of communication simply means a process of reducing messages into writing which is extensively used in organizations. Formal communication must always be in writing such as rules, orders, manuals, policy matters etc.

The systematic filing of written communication is one of the important aspects of communication. Filing along with indexing is necessary because of the poor retention power of human beings. The purpose of preserving written messages is to provide necessary information readily and without any delay and when it is needed. However, the following gives the main purpose of writing the messages.

> **Future references:** The limitation of the human mind and poor retention power cannot be overlooked. Written messages can be preserved as records and reference sources. Various media of communication can be filed for future reference. Thus, keeping records is essential for the continuous operation of the business.
>
> **Avoiding mistakes:** In transmitting messages, earlier records help in reducing mistakes and errors and also prevent the occurrence of fraud.

- **Legal requirements:** Written communication is acceptable as a legal document. That is why some executives think that even if some messages have been transmitted orally, they should later be confirmed in writing.

- **Wide access:** Communication media has become very fast, and written communication enjoys wide access. If the communicator and the receiver are far from each other, written communication sent through post or e-mail is the cheapest and may be the only available means of communication between them.

- **Effective decision-making:** old documents help effective decision-making in a great way. Decision-making process becomes easier if old records are available. Because the messages provide the necessary information for decision-making purpose.

PRESENTATION

Successful presenting consists of three elements:

Content: The presentation should be packed with practical and easy-to-remember information. Inject enthusiasm about the topic into your presentation through your voice and body language. Ask the audience questions so they have to keep awake, think and answer, delegates like to give answers. Also, try to include one or two exercises to get them thinking and joining in. Keep your presentation to the point and practice it to make sure that it lasts the length of time you are allotted to speak, taking into consideration question-and-answer time if appropriate. Always remember that you may miss out on something you intended to say but the audience will never know that you missed it so don't worry about it. Tell short stories to bring your presentation to life (these may be humorous) but be careful about telling jokes as they can seem out of place.

Confidence: Remember that some people get nervous in audiences too. You can put them at their ease by showing with your body language that you are confident of your ability; let them realize they will enjoy the forthcoming presentation. Knowing that you have information to share that is valuable for others also gives you confidence and satisfaction. Confidence will come with practice and with performing and being successful.

Practice: It is extremely important to write your presentation and practice, practice, practice until you can give it with ease. It is a well-known fact that the audience will only remember 7 percent of the words you say; 93 percent of what they will remember is your attitude, tone of voice and your physical presentation skills.

Once you know your presentation thoroughly, you then have to concentrate on how to give it in the most effective and memorable way you can. Make a connection with the audience by eye contact and drawing them into the message you wish to give by making it alive and interesting. Then the audience will be listening to every word and waiting to hear what you have to say next. You can use your experiences and anecdotes to help people remember the points you are making. You can also use a mnemonic to link key messages together.

PRESS CONFERENCE

Press conference is called when an organization has something newsworthy to tell to the media, and when more in-depth approach and discussion is needed then it is possible to provide by sending out a press release. There are two major reasons for holding a news conference. One is so that a newsmaker who gets many questions from reporters can answer them all at once rather than answering dozens of phone calls. Another is so someone can try to attract news coverage for something that was not of interest to journalists before. In a news conference, one or more speakers may make a statement, which may be followed by questions from reporters. Sometimes only questioning occurs, sometimes there is a statement with no questions permitted. Press conference gives reporters a possibility to ask questions, get explanations, quotes, and photo opportunity. While organizing press conference following points should be kept in the mind:

An invitation to the conference should be sent to reporters and desk editors a week ahead of it. Closer to the date a day or two before it a phone call can be made to remind the reporters on the event.

You should organize press conference between 9-11 in morning or 4-7 in evening. Later then or before that is not good - reporters will not have time to file a story for the next day newspaper issue.

Ideally, the conference will have several persons participating: the press officer who knows the reporters will open and facilitate it. One or two prominent persons should be present, who will give a 10-min statement each on the issue (project, release, donation, opening, or similar), after which the facilitator will give floor to the reporters to ask questions. All in all, ideally it should be finished in 45 min. After that individual interviews can be given.

A "press kit" is usually distributed at a conference, containing a press release, background of organizers, report, research results, fact sheets, list of experts, etc. Sometimes even filmed material or photo material is distributed. After the conference you should send the press kit by a messenger to those media outlets that have not sent a representative at the conference.

Reporters like to say that "A press conference should scream for a headline" meaning there should be breaking news released on them. If a conference is called and there is no such news, journalists will not forget it. There is a chance that next time, even if you have breaking news, nobody will show up at the event.

Exactly because of the proliferation of press conferences, media outlets often send beginners to cover them.

If possible, media events should be organized instead of press conference. Yet, if one decides to organize a press conference, there are a number of technical details to be taken care of.

Conference

A conference is closed group discussion. A conference is usually a large gathering of persons who meet to confer on a particular theme or to exchange experience or information. A conference may be held to exchange views on some problem being faced by the organization or some other issue related to it, and it may even suggest a solution, but the suggestions from a conference are not binding. They are more in the nature of recommendations. The participants in the conference have to register for attending the conference.

Within the organization, the sales manager may hold a weekly conference of the salesmen to review sales during the week and to plan the next week's strategy on the basis of the views expressed by them. Conference may sometimes be held to give training to new employees. These employees may be exposed to a conference where necessary information about the organization is imparted to them and through discussion in an informal atmosphere, they are made to learn all about the organization, its objectives, policies, etc. This kind of conference may be described as a conference for training. Occasionally a large industrial concern may take initiative and invite delegates from other similar concerns to a conference to discuss problem of mutual interest. The host organization selects the venue of the conference, makes arrangements for the stay of the delegates, chalks out detailed program, invite eminent people to chair various sessions, selects the speakers, and at the end of the conference sends out reports to leading newspapers highlighting some of the important aspects of the conference.

GLOSSARY

Acceptance testing: Formal testing conducted to determine whether or not a system satisfies its pre-defined acceptance criteria, and to enable the customer to determine whether or not to accept the system.

Accepted: The recorded decision or formal sign-off by the customer that an output has satisfied the documented requirements and may be delivered to the customer or used in the next part of the process.

Activity: An element of work performed during the course of a project. Normally has duration, expected cost, and expected resource requirements. Also called a work item.

Amount at stake: The extent of adverse consequences which could occur to the project. Also referred to as risk impact.

Application Developers: Application Developers include all those responsible for developing prototypes, technical specifications, and application code, and for executing test scripts

Assumptions: Assumptions are factors that, for planning purposes, will be considered to be true, real or certain. Assumptions generally involve a degree of risk and also should be reflected in the Risk Management plan.

Authorized: The recorded decision that a deliverable or output has been cleared for use after having satisfied the quality standards for the project.

Business Analyst: The Business Analyst effectively leads discussions with the Customers to determine the business requirements, participates in preparing the data and process models, prepares module specifications, test data, and user documentation materials, assists in prototyping activities and together with the Project Team develops strategies for testing and implementation.

Baseline Metrics: A set of indicators to set as measures against which to judge and report progress or performance.

Business Case: A one-off, start-up document used by corporate management to assess the justification of a proposed project, or to assess the development options for a project that has already received funding. If approved, it confirms corporate management support funding for a recommended course of action.

Business Customer: There may be other Business Units who will utilize the project outputs, but who do not have management responsibility for their ongoing maintenance or for the realization of outcomes/benefits. These are known as the Business Customers. Sometimes the Project Observer or the Project Business Owner represents the interests of the Business Customer.

Business Owner: The Business Owner is responsible for managing the project outputs for utilization by the Customers. There may be one or more Business Owner, at a number of managerial levels, depending on the size of the project. The Business Owners must be satisfied that the project includes all of the outputs necessary for outcome/benefits realization. Each output must be specified and delivered fit-for-purpose. Usually, the Business Owner is accountable to the Project Sponsor or their delegates, who may be Senior Management staff, for the realization of project Target Outcomes. One or more Business Owners are usually Steering Committee members.

The Business Owner must be identified for all projects, no matter what the size or complexity, even if they are the same entity as the Project Sponsor, or indeed the Project Manager.

Change Control Board: A formally constituted group of stakeholders responsible for approving or rejecting changes to the project baselines.

Constraints: Factors that will limit the project management team's options. For example, a predefined budget, deadlines, technology choices, scope or legislative processes.

Consultant: An organization or individual contracted to provide high-level specialist or professional advice to assist decision-making by management. Consultants will be expected to exercise their own skills and judgment independently.

Contingency Planning: The development of a management plan that identifies alternative strategies to be used if specified risk events occur.

Contingency Reserve: The amount of money or time needed above the estimate (project budget) in order to reduce the risk of overruns of project objectives to a level acceptable to the organization.

Contract: An agreement for the provision of goods and/or services, between two or more parties, intended to create a legal obligation between them and to be legally enforceable.

Contractor: An organization or individual contracted to provide a specialized service. A contractor will usually work under the supervision of a Project Manager to provide services that are not readily available.

Corporate Client: The high-level champion of the project who has ultimate authority. They promote the benefits of the project to the community.

Cost of Conformance: The cost of conforming to Specifications, Planning, Training, Control, Validation, Test, and Audits.

Cost Benefit Analysis: The economic justification for a proposed project.

Critical Path: The chain of activities that link the start to the finish of the project, and for which any delay will cause the project to be delayed by the same amount of time. The longest time taken by the project team to complete a project activity is the critical path.

Customer: The person or entities that will utilize the project outputs to generate the outcomes. See also Business Owner and Business Customer.

Database Administrator: Database Administrator is responsible for providing and maintaining database administration policies and procedures, approving and executing database scripts, performing database tuning activities, and transforming a pictorial representation of the system data (the Logical Data Model) into physical database tables that support the final system.

Data Process Modeler: Data Process Modeler develops and maintains data and process models to represent the business information needs in the area under study, develops and defines the data dictionary, validates models with the Customers, and participates in prototyping.

Decision Tree Analysis: A diagram that describes a decision under consideration and the implications of choosing one or another of the available alternatives. It incorporates probabilities or risks and the costs of each logical path of events and future decisions.

Deliverable: A tangible, verifiable work output, such as a Feasibility Study, a detailed design, a working prototype, any report, manual, specification, programming or other output, developed as part of a project. Usually a component of a high-level output descriptor.

Document Control: All documents, whether electronic or hard copy, need to be uniquely identifiable. In most cases, it is also necessary to track the changes that occur to the document and record its distribution throughout the document's development and subsequent revision(s). Document control includes:

- The use of version numbers on documents (version control)

- Maintaining a history of the development of versions (build status)
- The use of numbered copies of documents (controlled documents)
- Maintaining a list of recipients for distributed copies (distribution list)

Expected Monetary Value: The product of an event's probability of occurrence and the gain or loss that will result. Expected Monetary Value = Money at Risk x Probability. For example, if there is a 50% probability it will rain, and rain will result in a $100 loss, the expected monetary value of the rain event is $50 (.5 * $100).

Facilitator: The facilitator leads sessions to identify business requirements and issues, keep meeting sessions focused and productive, draws out issues and ideas from all participants, and maintains clear and open communications within the session.

Fast Tracking: Compressing the project schedule by overlapping activities that would normally be done in sequence (such as design and construction).

Feasibility Report: A report that is developed as a result of a Feasibility Study, and is presented to senior management to determine whether a project has sufficient merit to continue into more detailed phases. Refer Feasibility Study

Feasibility Study: A study to assess the viability of a potential project. It includes a cost/benefit analysis and results in the development of a Feasibility Report.

Fitness-for-purpose: The features by which the quality of an output is determined. In other words, what criteria will be used to test whether the outputs meet the needs of the project's Business Owner(s) and Customers, and will, in turn, enable outcomes to be realized

Gantt chart: Horizontal bar charts that can graphically depict the time relationship of tasks, activities and resources in a project.

Governance: The management structure created for the life of a project. Refer to Governance Model and Governance Structure

Governance Model: A generic model that indicates the people most likely to be incorporated in a project governance structure. It is also an indication of some of the ways in which the people would be most likely to interact.

Implementation Plan: Describes how the outputs will be delivered to the Business Owner(s), including any special requirements such as stage implementation or 'roll out', training and delivery requirements.

ISO Standards: The International Standards Organization (ISO) has developed a set of international standards that can be used in any type of business, and are accepted around the world as proof that a business can provide assured quality.

Issue: A concern raised by any stakeholder that needs to be addressed, either immediately or during the project. As issues are reviewed during the project, they may become a threat to the project and a mitigation strategy prepared. They are usually documented in a Project Issues Register.

Management Reserve: A separately planned quantity used to allow for future situations which are impossible to predict. Management reserves are intended to reduce the risk of missing cost or schedule objectives. Use of management reserves requires a change to the project's cost baseline. Management reserves are not included in the project's cost and schedule baseline. Also used to manage "unknown unknowns" types of risk.

Milestone: A significant scheduled event that acts as a progress marker in the life of a project. A milestone is either passed or it is not, the achievement or non-achievement of which is monitored and reported.

Mitigation: Taking steps to lessen risk by lowering the probability of a risk event's occurrence or reducing its effect should it occurs

Non-Key Stakeholder: Stakeholders who do not need to be recognized in order for the project to be successful, but who will be identified as a result of the process of identifying all stakeholders.

Outcome: The benefits and other long-term changes that are sought from undertaking a project. Project outcomes are achieved from the utilization of the outputs delivered by a project.

Output: The services or products resulted from a Process. It is delivered to the Business Owner(s) by the project.

Performance Measures: Criteria for measuring a project's success, whether the project is under control and the level of adherence to documented plans, methodologies and standards.

Phase: A section of work in a project for which there are no measurable outcomes at the end, although some outputs may be produced. Large and/or complex projects often scope the work in phases to enable each phase to be planned in more detail on completion of the previous phase.

Post Implementation Review: A review of a completed project. It may be a review of one or more aspects of the project. For example, whether the outcomes (benefits) were realized, the fitness-for-purpose of the outputs produced or the project and quality management processes selected and applied.

Program: A group of related projects that are managed in a coordinated fashion to support the organization strategic goals. E.g., a transformation program comprised of several projects that are implemented together to achieve the program objectives.

Project: A project brings about change and involves a group of inter-related activities that are planned and then executed in a certain sequence, to create a unique product or service (output) within a specific timeframe so that outcomes are achieved.

Project Issues Register: A list of all issues, details of how these issues are being managed and their current status.

Project Risk Management: Includes the processes concerned with identifying, analyzing, and responding to project risk.

Project Charter: A formal document issued by senior management which explains the purpose of the project including the business need the project addresses and the resulting product. It provides the project manager with the authority to apply organizational resources to project activities.

Project Brief: The Project Brief is a specific purpose document outlining what is to occur in the Initiation Phase of a project. A Project Brief is particularly useful where an output, which will result in a decision to proceed or not with the proposed project, is to be delivered from this initial phase. It also may be used instead of a small Project Business Plan for small projects.

Project Business Plan: The high-level management document for the project. It is owned, maintained and utilized by the Steering Committee to ensure the delivery of project outputs and the realization of defined project outcomes.

Project Management: Project Management is a formalized and structured method of managing a project using a standard processes, tools, and techniques guided by a comprehensive project management body of knowledge. It focuses on achieving specifically defined outputs that are to be achieved by a certain time, to a defined quality and with a given level of resources so that planned outcomes are achieved.

Project Management Framework: The formalized structure, processes and tools employed by an organization or enterprise to the management of all projects.

Project Management Methodology: A pre-defined set of tasks that are designed to provide a guide or a checklist for developing and implementing projects.

Project Team: The members of the project team who are directly involved in project management activities. On some smaller projects, the project management team may include virtually all of the project team members. The Project Team consists of a Project Manager and a variable number of Project Team members who are responsible for planning and executing the project.

Project Manager: The Project Manager is contracted by the Steering Committee to deliver the defined project outputs. The Project Manager is the person who is responsible for ensuring that the Project Team completes the project. The Project Manager develops the Project Management plan with the team and manages the team's performance. It is also the responsibility of the Project Manager to secure acceptance and approval of deliverables from the Project Sponsor and Stakeholders.

Project Metrics: Measures used to indicate progress or achievement of a project.

Project Observer: The Project Observer can be present at Steering Committee meetings or Project Team meetings to act as an information channel to the Agency they are representing. They usually have no voting rights.

Project Outcomes Review: A review of a project, involving as many project participants as possible, to assess if the desired outcomes/benefits were attained.

Project Output Review: A review of a project, involving as many project participants as possible, to evaluate the fitness-for-purpose of the outputs, the amount of deviation that occurred from the original specifications requested by the customer and the final result, and how any changes to these specifications were managed and approved.

Refer to Project Outcomes Review and Post Implementation Review

Project Phase: Refer to Phase

Project Portfolio Management: The management of prioritized projects within the organization, Business Unit, Agency or across government. It is a dynamic process requiring re-prioritization, as necessary, to meet changing business requirements or emerging opportunities.

Project Proposal: The initial document that converts an idea or policy into the details of a potential project, including the outcomes/benefits, outputs, major risks, costs, stakeholders and an estimate of the resourcing and time required.

Project Schedule: A detailed plan of major project phases, milestones, activities, tasks and the resources allocated to each task. The most common representation of the project schedule is the Gantt chart.

Project Scope: The work that must be done in order to deliver a product with the specified features and functions.

Project Sponsor: The Project Sponsor has ultimate accountability and responsibility for the project and is a member of the Steering Committee, usually the Chair. The Sponsor oversees the business management and project management issues that arise outside the formal business of the Steering Committee. The Sponsor also lends support by advocacy at a senior level and ensures that the necessary resources (both financial and human) are available to the project. The Corporate Client and Project Sponsor may be the same person for some projects.

Project Stakeholder: An individual or group whose interest in the project must be recognized if the project is to be successful. In particular, those who may be positively or negatively affected during the project or on successful completion the project.

Project Status Report: A regular report on the status of the project, with regard to project performance, milestones, budget, issues, risks and areas of concern, to the appropriate people.

Project Team: The Project Team is a group that is responsible for planning and executing the project. It consists of a Project Manager and a number of Project Team Members who are brought in to deliver their tasks according to the Project Schedule. The Project Team is led by the Project Manager, working for the successful delivery of the project outputs, as outlined in the Project Management plan. It is desirable that the Project Team includes representatives from the Business Units associated with the project. The composition of the Team may change as the project moves through its various phases. The assessment and selection of people with the requisite skills required for each phase of a project is critical to its overall success. The skills should be explicitly identified as a part of the System Design process. The Project Team is responsible for completing tasks and activities required for delivering project outputs.

Project Team Member: The Project Team Member is led by the Project Manager working for the successful delivery of the project outputs. Project Team Member is responsible for executing tasks and producing deliverables as outlined in the Project Management plan and directed by the Project Manager, at whatever level of effort or participation has been defined for him/her.

Project Management plan: A formal approved document used to guide both System Construction and System Acceptance activities. The primary uses of the Project Management plan are to document planning assumptions and decisions, to facilitate communication among stakeholders, and to document approved scope, cost, and schedule baselines.

Project Quality Management: The processes required ensuring that the project will satisfy the needs for which it was undertaken. Modern quality management complements modern project management in that both recognize the importance of customer satisfaction and prevention over inspection.

Procurement Plan: Provides a detailed plan of the process for acquiring the proposed goods and services to support the delivery of the project's outputs.

Quality Assurance: The application of planned, systematic activities, within a documented management framework, that provides confidence that the outputs from a process meet the Customer's requirements.

Quality Assurance Analyst: QA Analyst is responsible for establishing and executing the Quality Assurance Plan, for assisting in the preparation of test scripts and test data, and for participating in integration and acceptance testing efforts

Quality Control: The process of monitoring the adherence to documented quality assurance procedures.

Quality Management: Quality management is the policy and associated procedures, methods and standards required for the control of projects. The purpose of quality management is to increase certainty by reducing the risk of project failure. It also provides the opportunity for continuous improvement.

Quality Management System: Defined policies and procedures that provide a formal framework describing the way an organization conducts its core business. The performance of each quality management procedure generates objective evidence by which to measure the performance of the organization and its management.

Quality Plan: Also commonly called the Quality Management plan. It summarizes the quality management approach and how it will support the delivery of the project outputs.

Residual Risk: A risk that remains after risk responses have been implemented.

Reference Group: A committee that provides forums to achieve consensus among groups of stakeholders. Often provides expert advice on the development of project outputs. There may be more than one Reference Group for large projects.

Resources: The people, finances, physical and information resources required to perform the project activities.

Risk: Any factor (or threat) that may adversely affect the successful completion of the project. They are usually documented in a Risk Register.

Risk Assessment: Undertaking a process to assess identified threats to the success of the project, which results in working papers of the current assessment for each threat (both likelihood and seriousness), a risk grading and strategies for mitigating the risks. The results of this analysis are usually captured in the Risk Register.

Risk Management: Describes the processes concerned with identifying, analyzing and responding to project risk. It consists of risk identification, risk analysis, risk evaluation and risk treatment. The processes are iterative throughout the life of the project.

Risk Management plan: A detailed plan describes the proposed risk management approach for the project.

Risk Register: A document that records the results of a risk analysis process. It includes the identified threats to the success of the project, the current assessment for each threat (both likelihood and seriousness), a risk grading and strategies for mitigating the risks.

Risk Response plan: A document detailing all identified risks, including description, cause, the probability of occurrence, impacts on objectives, proposed responses, owners, and current status. Also known as the risk register.

Scope: A clear statement of the areas of impact and boundaries of the project. The scope of a project includes the Target Outcomes, other benefits, customers, outputs, work and resources (both financial and human).

Scope Statement: A documented description of the project as to its output, approach, and content. (What is being produced? How is it being produced? and What is included?)

Scope Creep: Any modification to the scope of a project that has not been authorized or approved by the appropriate individual or group.

Slippage: The extent to which the project is falling behind time in relation to the Project Development Schedule.

Stage: A major segment of a project for which there are outputs and outcomes at the end.

Stakeholder Management plan: Identifies and summarizes stakeholder involvement, including identification of stakeholders for related projects.

Stakeholder: A person or organization that has an interest in the project processes, outputs or outcomes. Refer to Key Stakeholder(s) and Non-Key Stakeholder(s)

Steering Committee: A Steering Committee is the key body within the governance structure that is responsible for the business issues associated with the project. It is essential to ensuring the delivery of the project outputs and the achievement of project outcomes/benefits. Its responsibilities include approving the budgetary strategy, defining and realizing benefits, monitoring risks, quality and timelines, making policy and resourcing decisions, and assessing requests for changes to the scope of the project.

Target Outcome(s): The measurable benefits that are sought from undertaking a project. Target Outcomes are achieved from the utilization of the outputs delivered by a project. Stated, identified targets and measures are developed for gauging progress towards their achievement.

Technical Architect: Technical Architect drives the logical process and data models into an application architecture, establishes architecture guidelines, and develops strategies for the creation and distribution of applications.

Technical Services: include all those responsible for the ordering, installation and maintenance of hardware and software components, LAN/WAN components and telecommunications components.

Technical Support: includes all those responsible for supporting the development of the new system. Support includes the documentation of user, training, operation materials, and help files, training for Customers, responding to technical and business questions forwarded to the Help Desk, and supporting the project and associated administrative processes

Test Plan: A detailed plan that addresses all aspects related to the test of an output or sub-output. It should include test scenarios, the test schedule and define any necessary support tools.

Test Specification: Describes the test criteria and the methods to be used in a specific test to assure the performance and design specifications have been satisfied. The test specification identifies the capabilities or program functions to be tested and identifies the test environment. It may include test data to support identified test scenarios.

Testing: The process of exercising or evaluating an output, such as an IT system or system component, by manual or automated means, to confirm that it satisfies specified requirements or to identify differences between expected and actual results.

Version Control: A control or identification system for documents, outputs and sub-outputs, enabling stakeholders to identify readily each different release.

Work Breakdown Structure: It refers to the breaking down of the work in a project into related tasks.

AUTHOR BIOGRAPHY

Dr Zulk Shamsuddin, PhD, AMC®, CIPT, MPM®
Accredited Management Consultant®
Chartered International Professional Trainer
Master Project Manager®

    Dr. Zulk is a technology and business consultant with skills and experience in learning and development, project management, risk management, design, and delivery of strategic training programs including facilities management for knowledge, career development and professional skills certifications. A certified trainer and certification counsellor of The American Academy of Project Management ® AAPM and the Global Academy of Finance and Management ® GAFM. Dr. Zulk is a senior member of the global advisory Board and the International Board of Standards.

Join Dr. Zulk international network at PMI Community

https://community.pmi.org/profile/zulkhernain

www.ingramcontent.com/pod-product-compliance
Lightning Source LLC
Chambersburg PA
CBHW071652240526
45469CB00021B/1996